T0304911

A Pocket Guide to Nike
Josh Sims

A Pocket Guide to Nike

Josh Sims

Laurence King

Contents

Introduction

When Phil Knight first thought about going into
business in the early 1960s, it was, he assumed,
always going to be a niche one. This was a time
when running for fitness away from the athletics
track – jogging – was still considered oddball; and
when the US had no real history of making sports
shoes (Converse basketball boots aside). That's
why Knight first set out to import sports shoes from
Japan. But his company, Blue Ribbon Sports, grew
faster than expected. Within seven years it had
fifty employees, running for fitness was less
strange and the arrangement Knight had with his
Japanese supplier was winding down. Perhaps, he
wondered, now was the time to start making his
own shoes.

Yet the idea that the company he was building
would become a global monolith did not occur to
him. Indeed, when he put in his first order of shoes
Knight hadn't even thought of a name for what
struck him as being a new beginning. Jeff Johnson,
Blue Ribbon Sports' first employee, suggested a
name last-minute. How about Nike – pronounced
'nike-ee', though so often mispronounced – after
the Greek goddess of victory?

To say that Nike would become a phenomenon would be an understatement. It would become the US's biggest sportswear company, and then the world's. It would rewrite the rules of sports marketing and sponsorship. It would prove a pioneer in materials and design technology in the pursuit of lighter, stronger, more functional footwear and, latterly, clothing, too. But it would also pioneer the blurring of sport with street culture and fashion, inspiring an entire sneaker-collecting economy that is now taken for granted. Lastly, it would become a household name even in homes with no interest in sport, fashion or design.

As enthusiastic runners, Knight and his Nike co-founder, Bill Bowerman, only set out to make better running shoes. What they created was a cultural and corporate giant. The name Nike could hardly have been more apt.

History

It was in 1971 that the first shoe carrying the Nike name arrived in stores, even if the company behind it would not do so for another seven years. Until then, what has since become a global brand was known, less snappily, as Blue Ribbon Sports. The company had been founded in 1964 by Philip Knight with William (Bill) Bowerman, Knight's one-time track and field coach at the University of Oregon – the city where the company still has its headquarters.

Initially, Blue Ribbon Sports was the exclusive importer of high-quality running shoes made by the

Japanese company Onitsuka Tiger, albeit initially just sold from the trunk of Knight's car. But growth was fast and in 1966 the brand opened its first shop, in Santa Monica. The idea of making its own shoes wasn't, at that stage, something it planned – for all that Bowerman had been tinkering with his own shoe designs.

That is, until the sprinter Otis Davis – who had deformed feet and needed custom running shoes – wore a pair of Bowerman's design to win Olympic gold in the 400m in Rome in 1960. Blue Ribbon

ABOVE: Otis Davis winning gold in the 400m in the Rome Olympic Games in 1960.

ABOVE: Bill Bowerman (in the hat), track and field coach at the University of Oregon and co-founder of Nike.

Sports had, until that moment, just wanted to offer the best running shoes it could find. It turned out the best it could find, they would come to conclude, could be bettered.

Bowerman – who split his runners into what he called 'tigers' and 'hamburgers', tigers being the elite athletes, the fighters – wanted to give them something that would make them fight harder still.

He was a coach with a tough-love style: 'You have to choose between becoming a good athlete or a good lover,' he told his male charges (women still being largely excluded from college athletics, let alone major competitions). In other words, there was no time for romance if you were serious about track.

It turned out the best running shoes Blue Ribbon Sports could find . . . could be bettered.

Knight was already attuned to the idea of how a new generation of products could outclass what had come before, no matter how well-established and respected. While an MBA student at Stanford University (he graduated in 1962) Knight had written a paper with the title 'Can Japanese sports shoes do to German sports shoes what Japanese cameras did to German cameras?' Just two decades after Pearl Harbor and the US's subsequent entry into the Second World War, Japan was in the spotlight, undergoing an economic miracle and newly fashionable, thanks to the Manga, interior style and electronics that were now seeping into the US market. The US government, keen to present Japan as an ally now, leaned on its PR machine to this effect. Knight even flirted with Buddhism.

But Knight's business was, for him, still more about how he might improve running shoes. After all, these really mattered to those who wore them. Knight headed to Japan right after graduation and, following his nose, wandered into a sports shoe shop. Not long after, he tracked down the owner of Onitsuka Tiger, Kihachiro Onitsuka, and convinced him he could open the US market for the brand. Almost a year later, around 300 pairs of shoes arrived in Portland. Knight showed these 'flats' – running shoes without spikes – to Bowerman and he was impressed. So much so that a few months later they agreed to both put US$500 into a new business together, named for the ribbon broken by winners in a race.

'Shoes are the one important piece of equipment for a runner,' Knight would later say in an interview with CNN, regarding Bowerman's determination to improve on what Japan could supply – and all the more so as relations with Onitsuka Tiger slowly soured. He continued: 'If it's baseball, it's the ball and mitt. But for runners, it's shoes and that's it. And my old coach [Bowerman] firmly believed that an ounce in a pair of shoes over the last quarter of a mile was worth ten thousand pounds over the last three yards. He was obsessed [with that kind of detail]. That got my attention and I became a guinea pig of his own experimental shoes.'

Knight was not alone. As a university coach, Bowerman had the perfect testing ground: some 50 college athletes ready to try anything he made

for them. He would x-ray their feet to work out
the best positioning for spikes along a shoe's sole.
He would experiment with different forms of
cushioning, investigate the ways shoes interacted
with track surfaces, explore ideas about energy
drinks and test different fabrics for runner's clothing,
proposing parachute silk for its super-light weight
and prefiguring now-standard nylon shorts by
some decades.

The Nike Waffle, famously, had a sole that originated
from Bowerman pouring melted urethane into his
wife's waffle iron – albeit forgetting to add some
non-stick agent onto it first – to create a slimline,
lightweight unit with plenty of grip. This grip was said
to leave a distinct imprint on the ground, thereby
winning the style the nickname 'Moon Shoe'.
Here was a company, it would state in an early
advertisement, 'not bound by tradition or long,
profitable production runs [which is to say that it
would release new styles as fast as innovation
allowed]. We've combined the best features of the
old shoes with the newest ideas of the best athletes.'

Knight has said that he was acutely aware that
succeeding with their own line of shoes – given the
competition and the then small market for running
shoes – was 'a long shot'. That's why he continued
his training not just at the track, but also as an
accountant, much to his father's relief. His father,
of course, need not have worried – as an indicator

ABOVE: Early example of Nike athletic shoes, with Bowerman's 'waffle' sole design.

of the stupendous growth of Nike, an early pair of those Nike Waffles (specifically a 1972 Moon Shoe version) would sell at auction via Sotheby's in 2019 for US$437,500, while Nike would come to be valued at over US$100 billion.

A New Name

Nike was very nearly not called Nike at all. A number of names were considered. According to Geoff Hollister in his book *Out of Nowhere* (2008), Knight liked the idea of Dimension Six, inspired by his love of the pop group The 5th Dimension. Knight said: 'There was a 5th dimension, right? So we wanted [the new business] to be the extra dimension . . . [But] you'd have a hard time fitting that [name] on a heel tab. Just think where we would be if I picked that name.' Blue Ribbon Sports had 45 employees at the time and everyone put a name into a hat.

Some employees suggested emulating the German sports brand Puma; Jeff Johnson consequently suggested Peregrine. Another suggested Bengal.

It was Johnson who came up with Nike in 1971. He was said to have been inspired by an article in an inflight magazine that analyzed how many successful brands had one- or two-syllable names with a Z, X or K in them (like Xerox or Kleenex). The response was lacklustre. Johnson was told, 'Nobody liked it, but it seemed better than anything else.' Knight wasn't keen either: 'I don't like any of [the name suggestions], but I guess it's the best of the bunch.'

> ### *Many successful brands had one- or two-syllable names with a Z, X or K in them.*

That was very much the Knight way: not waiting for the perfect solution, if something good enough allowed progress to be made. 'Nothing ever stands out [for me] and says, "Boy, that's it!" There's not a eureka moment for me,' he said to CBS in 2016. 'In almost all these things I just say, "Okay, that's the best we can do – let's go."'

Knight's pragmatic approach saved time, allowing Nike to press on towards the showcase that would be the 1972 Munich Olympics. In 1971 Knight – having experienced the limitations of being locked into an exclusive deal with Onitsuka Tiger – had begun to establish a network of subcontractors across Japan, giving him greater control. That was the year before Blue Ribbon Sports' contract with Onitsuka Tiger had expired – and both sides have since claimed the other was at fault: Onitsuka Tiger that Nike was operating in contravention of their deal; Nike that Onitsuka Tiger was trying to get out of the exclusivity arrangement.

Either way, clearly Knight was itching to get ahead. In 1974 Nike opened a manufacturing plant in Exeter, New Hampshire, in 1976 it established a production line in Taiwan, then another in South Korea the following year. Remarkably, by 1978, the year that the official switch was made from Blue Ribbon Sports to Nike, Nike shoes had been worn by Jon Anderson to win the Boston Marathon, Jimmy Connors to win both the US Open and Wimbledon, Henry Rono to set four new track and field records, as well as by members of both the Los Angeles Lakers and Boston Celtics basketball teams – all these sports professionals embracing the new brand.

Two years later, Nike opened its first research and development lab and began pondering ways of trapping a bubble of air into a sole. Nike would not

RIGHT: Jimmy Connors in the 1975 Wimbledon final.

only register more patents than any other footwear company, but it would also become one of the fastest-growing companies in American corporate history. In 1980 it was able to make its first sale of shares to the public – listing on the stock exchange the same fortnight as a fledgling tech company by the name of Apple – making Knight and Bowerman multi-millionaires. By 1989, Nike was the largest sportswear company in America.

And this was all before it had really tapped the market that made it a phenomenon beyond sport. Although Nike would not deliberately embrace the leisure market for many years to come – it saw itself strictly as a sports brand for sportspeople – nonetheless, its experience in Los Angeles might have shown the company's direction of travel. Throughout the 1980s, Hollywood stuntmen bought Nike shoes, as did costume designers for movies; American actor Paul Newman is said to have started wearing them, the rock bands the Rolling Stones and the Ramones, too.

Launching Nike was not all easy. The Oregon-born Knight has noted that in the 1960s there was considerably less red tape than would prove the case over subsequent decades. His first office was

RIGHT: Nikes were worn in *The Goonies* (1985) and *Karate Kid* (1984).

his Plymouth Valiant, and he sold Blue Ribbon Sports' first shoes from its trunk, having got his sister to get a licence to do so from the town hall. In addition, there was no money – getting investors to put their money into Japanese track shoes was an especially tall order, as Knight has pointed out – and that was what kept Nike on the precipice of failure for a long time, no matter how successful it seemed from the outside.

Perhaps that's why the company was prepared to push at the limits of regulations. Paying Olympic athletes to wear its shoes was still not allowed – they were considered amateurs in the truest sense, unable to receive financial compensation in any form until 1972. But financing their travel was allowed. Nike would offer athletes' families a vacation in Hawaii or the Oregon resort town of Sunriver. Perks like these seemed, at the time, about the only thing runners could get from running, except the chance of glory.

In another workaround, shoes could be 'donated', too, so Nike did so generously: if Adidas gave its athlete friends two pairs of training shoes and a pair of spikes each year – which was extraordinary enough at the time – then Nike provided fresh pairs fortnightly, if that's what was wanted. In 1977 Nike

LEFT: The Ramones wearing Nike in 1984.

executive Rob Strasser hired Sonny Vaccaro (the marketing consultant who later helped to land the contract with Michael Jordan) for an unusual, perhaps ethically dubious but not illegal role: Vaccaro was given an envelope stuffed with US$30,000 with which to pay any university coaches who agreed to distribute Nike shoes to their players.

Some athletes needed no such encouragement. The French basketball player Richard Dacoury, for example, could choose Nike shoes cost-free when he joined his club Limoges in 1978. There was just one problem: Limoges was sponsored by Adidas. Dacoury's solution, before finally taking legal action against his club? He took every pair of Nike shoes he received to a local cobbler, had the Swoosh removed and three stripes sewn on.

Controversy

Certainly, the story of Nike has not been without controversy, particularly with regard to its labour practices. The company may have begun manufacturing its shoes in Japan but would later move production to South Korea and Taiwan, and then China, Vietnam and Indonesia, chasing lower costs. By the late 1990s, the company had some 100

RIGHT: American singer Billy Joel concert at Madison Square Garden in 1982.

subcontractors operating 500 production sites in more than 30 countries. Knight has noted that one reason for the company's early and rapid success was that it was good at keeping its manufacturing costs down by making its products in low-wage Asia, while its competitors, Adidas and Puma, were still manufacturing in high-wage European countries.

Nike was certainly not alone among major clothing and shoe brands in doing this – it became something of a whipping boy in this matter – but a report published in 1991 by activist labour group Press For Change's Jeff Ballinger put it under the spotlight by documenting poor working conditions at subcontracted Nike operations in Indonesia. Bad press followed, as did an angry public, with protests against Nike at the 1992 Olympics and on student campuses, with calls for a boycott.

Nike – whether it felt morally obliged to or forced against its will – responded by raising wages, monitoring factory conditions and enforcing clean-air standards. By the end of the 1990s, it had founded the Fair Labor Association and subsequently audited some 600 factories, publicly disclosing their locations in the process. However, as is the case for many apparel giants, Nike remained haunted by the human rights issues around manufacturing in the developing world. 'I think we made a lot of mistakes early on. Most of them due to the chief executive officer,' Knight has said. 'That was me.'

In what amounted to something of an about face, Nike even came to be seen as an industry leader among the giant brands in adopting more environmentally sound manufacturing. For example, it conducted an exhaustive chemical study of the threads and dyes that it used, eliminating from its manufacturing any that were found to be questionable. It also introduced innovations such as Flyknit, providing a less wasteful alternative to traditional cut-and-sewn ways of working with leather.

Of course, Nike has not been above using controversy to its own advantage either. In 2018 it signed Colin Kaepernick as its latest brand ambassador – the NFL player who had kicked up a storm by, during the national anthem, 'taking the knee' in acknowledgement of alleged police brutality towards Black Americans. His team, the 49ers, subsequently declined to renew his contract, and no other NFL team expressed interest. Kaepernick was either pariah or hero, depending on your point of view.

Knight has said that, privately, he was 'torn' on the question of taking the knee – he had himself served in the army and was a reservist for seven years, so maintained a traditional form of patriotism – but Nike proposed 'hero', making a show in backing Kaepernick as exemplary of high principle and independent-mindedness. 'Believe in something.

Even if it means sacrificing everything,' ran a Nike ad featuring Kaepernick.

'[Mark] Parker [the CEO of Nike at the time] looks at [the commercial] and went "Gulp!"' Knight would recall. He wasn't entirely wrong, either. Nike was subsequently accused of lacking in patriotism and faced another boycott, with some enraged customers taking to social media to burn their sneakers. As might be suspected, Nike knew what the result would be: during the following month its share price rocketed by over US$6 billion.

'It doesn't matter how many people hate your brand as long as enough people love it.'

As Knight would put it in a talk to Stanford Graduate School of Business students in 2019: 'It doesn't matter how many people hate your brand as long as enough people love it. You can't be afraid of offending people. You can't try and go down the middle of the road. You have to take a stand on something.'

RIGHT: Nike ad featuring Colin Kaepernick.

Nike is often noted as being one of the world's most recognizable brands – that's not just in the sporting goods world but among all brands. Yet coming to appreciate the importance of building that brand – of marketing, of public image – came late to the company. As Knight would stress, he and his team saw themselves as a group of runners obsessed with improving the experience of running for other runners. And that was all. They were about design and product – not building a profile or identity. That position, of course, would change – and in a major way.

The Swoosh

The story has it that the designer of Nike's globally recognizable 'Swoosh' logo was paid only US$35 for her efforts – cue outrage at the multi-billion-dollar company paying so little for something so important. But, of course, when Knight (then an accounting professor at Portland State University) approached Carolyn Davidson (then a student of graphic design at the university), Nike's big future was a long way ahead of it.

RIGHT: Nike brand advertising through the years.

MOVE MORE.
MOVE BETTER.
THE NIKE DRI-FIT KNIT TANK

JUST DO IT

JUST BUY IT
AT OLYMPUS SPORT

The U.K.'s No.1 sports retailer. Over 130 stores nationwide.

Touch

Everyone dances differently.
My way scores goals.
—Ronaldinho

IKE CHROM

JUST BECAUSE YOU'RE A
NICE GIRL DOESN'T MEAN YOU
CAN'T HAVE EVIL LEGS.

APPAREL

TAKE SPORT. ADD MUSK.

www.nikewomen.com

This was in 1971. Nike was planning its name change but was still called Blue Ribbon Sports and the company was just seven years old. And nobody really had money to splash around – Knight offered Davidson the work of 'writing some signs' for an hourly rate, after overhearing that she didn't have the money to pay for an oil-painting class.

'The price wasn't great at the time,' Davidson would tell *The Oregonian* in 1983, 'but they paid what I charged.' The job actually represented a golden opportunity for her to get real-world work experience. And later, in 1983, in recognition of the contribution that her design made, she would be presented with a diamond ring with a Swoosh engraving, a box of chocolates (Swoosh-shaped, of course) and some Nike stock. 'We plan to make that worth quite a lot,' Knight laughed at the time. Davidson would work on further graphic design projects for the company for some time after.

BELOW: The development of the Swoosh.

BLUE RIBBON SPORTS

1964

1972

The 'Swoosh' – as it would come to be called, with Nike even registering the word as a trademark – was designed to suggest a wing; the wing, perhaps, of Nike, the Greek goddess of victory after whom the company was renamed. But it was not an instant hit. Knight didn't like it much – he called it 'that big fat checkmark'. But – a testament to his business leadership style of bowing to others' expertise – he accepted that those more qualified did. 'I don't love it, but it will grow on me,' he said.

There was much in the logo's favour. It had a dynamism that chimed with the company's new name. Like the three bold lines of rival Adidas's logo, Nike's Swoosh outline was graphically simple, meaning it could be printed or embroidered easily and scaled up or down. In contrast, Knight had always been bothered by the Blue Ribbon Sports 'BRS' logo – the smaller it got, the harder it was to read. In later years, the Swoosh's very naivety meant

1978   1987   PRESENT

that it could be easily copied – not just by counterfeiters but also by the brand's superfans, in their doodles and even as tattoos.

Most importantly, the Swoosh went well up the side of a shoe – the key aspect of Knight's brief to Davidson – and its swooping curves suggested forward motion. It even circumvented the occasional amateur athletics rule. When the athlete Steve 'Pre' Prefontaine (Nike's first ambassador) was told to remove the four letters of the new brand he wore on his warm-up outfit, he returned in another emblazoned with this odd 'tick' graphic, to no questions.

'[Carolyn] was paid US$2 an hour and I never thought she would spend 17.5 hours on the project,' Knight

Nike's Swoosh outline was graphically simple.

joked at the ceremony at which Davidson was given her Nike stock. 'And when we gave her the US$35 [cheque], we asked her not to cash it right away.'

For that US$35 Knight got several designs – hundreds of iterations, Davidson has said – including that of the Swoosh, or the 'strip', as it was initially called within the company. It was first used with the word 'Nike' written over it, in script. But over the years, there was a growing acknowledgment that

the logo had become as culturally resonant as the company's name.

ABOVE: The Swoosh works well up the side of a shoe.

In 1978 the Swoosh, until then only an outline, was filled in to become a more imposing solid-black tick, with the Nike name also redesigned from a cursive font into a more eye-catching, defiant all-caps vision in Future Bold. In 1985 there was a colour change with both the brand name and the Swoosh in white against a red background. And in 1995 the brand name – until then used over the Swoosh or merged with it – was dropped altogether from the logo, leaving the Swoosh standing alone.

This was a commonplace move among global brands at the time – Shell and Apple both did similar, for example – but also made the Swoosh more versatile in terms of its placement on Nike goods. Freed of the need to state 'Nike' at all, now the Swoosh could be used in more creative ways. And that mattered to a company said to spend some 10 per cent of its annual revenue on marketing, relative to 3 per cent on manufacturing facilities and research and development. It was also, arguably, a learning experience for Nike. When its sponsorship deal with Michael Jordan was being pursued (see pages 67–71), it was quick to realize the potential of the basketball superstar to become a sub-brand in his own right – and so, accordingly, it developed the 'Jumpman' logo just for Jordan products.

Connecting with Athletes

Knight has conceded that Nike's fast and stratospheric success somewhat went to their heads and they made what were, in retrospect, some bad business decisions throughout a troubled 1980s. For example, it ploughed unsuccessfully into the aerobics market. It made a product that was in many ways superior to that of Reebok, but missing the styling that acknowledged aerobics was as much a lifestyle choice as a new means of exercise. Such was Nike's constitutional emphasis on technology, it decided that it needed to find a stronger and softer leather alternative to the garment leather being used by Reebok. But by the time it had done so, Reebok was established as the clear market leader.

Maybe worse still, Nike started to make casual shoes, damaging its close association with sports in the process. 'We got our brains beat out,' as Knight told the *Harvard Business Review* in 1992. 'We came out with a functional shoe we thought the world needed, but it was funny looking and the public didn't want it. Just because you have the best athletes in the world and a [logo] that everybody recognizes, doesn't mean you can take that trademark to the ends of the earth.'

'The way to stay ahead was through product innovation.'

Knight has said Nike had assumed that success was just down to the products it was creating for elite sportspeople, and that this alone was reason enough for anyone else to buy them. 'In the early days, anybody with a glue pot and a pair of scissors could get into the shoe business, so the way to stay ahead was through product innovation. We happen to be great at [that],' Knight has explained.

What Nike lacked, arguably, was what it would develop – a personality that was all about sports and fitness regardless of ability, that was about 'competition, determination, achievement, fun and even the spiritual rewards of participating in those activities,' as Knight explained. Nike had to learn to become inclusive, more human.

Surprisingly, given what a brand giant Nike would come to be, throughout most of the 1970s it did comparatively little marketing: most of its staff were runners, it understood running and recruited staff from the running track, and so it just focused on getting its shoes on runners' feet. Admittedly, these were world-class runners, the likes of Alberto Salazar and Steve Prefontaine, to whom, in 1974, Nike offered its first sponsorship contract, worth US$5,000 annually. This deal exposed the generation gap between Nike's co-founders, with the gentlemanly Bowerman perplexed by the very idea of using an ambassador to promote the

BELOW: Nike was slow to enter the aerobics market in the 1980s.

company's shoes. 'At no time did I authorize you to use the name or image of an athlete to promote [Nike] products,' Bowerman is said to have scolded Knight. 'That would be infringing on the rights of that young man.'

In 1972 Nike signed its first professional sports figure to an endorsement contract, the Romanian tennis champion Ilie Năstase, for just a season. But, generally, these deals were unlikely to entice the public into wearing Nike shoes. Nike took the same approach with each of the sports it developed shoes for – getting to know players and understanding their needs, then addressing those through design and product.

This honest approach – free of smoke and mirrors – was admirable in many ways. But, by aiming at sporting elites, Nike ignored the bulk of people who were wearing Nike shoes; even by the early 1970s, well over half of all the company's shoe sales were to people who were not using those shoes for the sport for which they were intended.

'If a top player like Michael Jordan liked some kind of yellow and orange jobbie, that's what we made, even if nobody else really wanted yellow or orange,' Knight has noted, citing the failure of the Sock Racer – a brilliant idea realized in a bright yellow that put everyone off. By the mid-1980s, Nike was recording losses and laying off staff. By the end of the decade, it would need to find its feet again.

'For years we thought of ourselves as a production-oriented company, meaning we put all of our emphasis on designing and manufacturing the product,' Knight has explained. 'But now we understand that the most important thing we do is market the product. We've come round to saying that Nike is a marketing-oriented company . . . We used to think that everything started in the lab. Now we realize everything spins off the consumer.'

One thing Nike learned was to slice up its produce into easily digestible chunks – in other words, it learned the art of the sub-brand. Air Jordan is the definitive example of this – powerful enough to stand apart from Nike itself. But even the basketball products would be further segmented – into Force and Flight – to better suit different playing styles. Similarly, tennis was divided into Challenge Court, as Knight has described it, 'very young, very anti-country club, very rebellious,' nonetheless making Nike the biggest brand in tennis; and Supreme Court, which recognized that tennis was still a mostly conservative sport.

Connecting with People

Unusually, Nike had become a billion-dollar company by 1980 without any TV advertising at all. The only magazines it advertised in were the likes of

RIGHT: Brazilian footballer Ronaldinho's skills have made him popular with fans and sponsors alike.

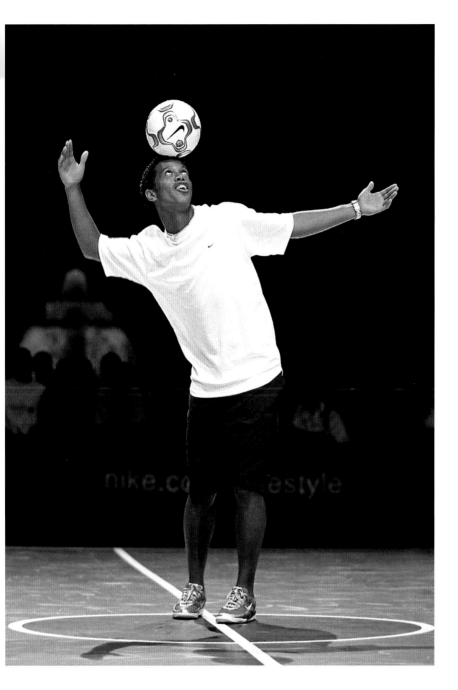

RIGHT: Michael Jordan's exceptional jumping ability would be echoed in his own 'Jumpman' Nike logo.

Runner's World. But then, in 1987, came its first TV commercial, what it called 'Visible Air' – the unveiling of the Air technology in a shoe through a window in its sole – set to the Beatles' 'Revolution' (1968). A year ahead of 'Just do it', one version of the ad started with an almost-familiar phrase: 'Do something. Anything.'

Much as Nike shoes marked a radical departure for sports shoe design, so their marketing was a radical departure for sports brand advertising. It showed normal people engaging in whatever fitness activity pleased them – cycling, lifting weights, playing ball; being determined but having fun – and was set, in a way almost unheard of until then, to a classic pop song by one of the biggest bands of all time.

The ad created a feeling – even if that came at a price. While Capitol Records and Yoko Ono – who managed John Lennon's estate – agreed to the song's use, the rest of the band did not. They sued for US$15 million, with Capitol Records settling in an

Are you
sick of
hearing
"where do
you find
the time"?

Is there a make-up kit in your gym bag?
Do you consider tri-athletes underachievers?
Does your kick-boxing trainer
make fun of your yoga instructor?
Have you ever done
crunches while waiting for pasta to cook?
Do you keep more than one pair of trainers
at work?

Are you an All Rounder?

Find yourself at
nikewomen.com

undisclosed deal. Nike's reaction? 'That made everything even more cool,' Nike designer Tinker Hatfield once recalled, 'because Yoko Ono got to fight with the rest of the Beatles. The whole thing hit the market and was like a rocket ship.'

'Take a chance and learn from it.'

An emotional connection had always been vital to Nike in choosing the athletes it wanted to work with, because it meant these would be the athletes that resonated with consumers. Now that feeling had to become part of its public image. 'The trick is to get athletes who not only can win but can stir up emotion, not just the leading scorer but someone the public is going to love or hate,' as Knight has explained in his memoir *Shoe Dog* (2016). Hence, for Nike, Arnold Palmer still trumps Jack Nicklaus, even if Nicklaus is the better golfer.

But then, 'We've always believed that to succeed with the consumer you have to wake him up,' Knight has noted. 'If you do the same thing you've done before or that somebody else is doing, you won't last more than one or two seasons. [That also means] we're

LEFT: Nike's direct appeal to women attempted to change perceptions that a dedication to sport was 'just for men'.

ABOVE: Michael Jordan in *Space Jam* (1996).

prepared for some criticism, because somebody will be offended no matter what we do. Our basic philosophy is: take a chance and learn from it.'

Take Nike's 'Hare Jordan' Super Bowl commercial in 1992: a million dollars in production costs and six months of animation work to show Michael Jordan playing basketball with, of all things, a cartoon character – Bugs Bunny. 'It could have been plain silly or just plain dumb,' Knight recognized of the ad, devised by Nike's long-time, Oregon-based advertising agency Wieden+Kennedy. Instead, the ad became a massive talking point, and three years later inspired a whole film, *Space Jam*, based around the same crazy premise – so crazy, in fact, that casting leading actors for it proved to be a major headache.

'Nike became strong because it wasn't just trying to peddle products,' Wieden+Kennedy founder Dan Wieden once noted. 'It was trying to peddle ideas and the mental and physical options you can take. [That] was really unusual.'

Just Do It

Often cited as the best tagline of the 20th century, three words – 'Just do it' – made for a direct, punchy, competitive advertising line. Part battle cry, part command, it was something people could just say to each other to capture a sense of drive and effort. It represented a kind of rebirth for Nike – a new focus on the brand and what it stood for – and came to grace countless t-shirts, bags and shoe boxes.

But these three words actually had an inauspicious beginning. In creating Nike's first multi-ad TV campaign, in 1988, Wieden+Kennedy had used different creative teams for the various sports portrayed in each of the five commercials, resulting in a mishmash of styles. This was something that suddenly occurred to Wieden while reviewing the commercials the evening before presenting them to Nike's board. The ads needed, he worried, something to pull them all together: a tagline.

Wieden was, no doubt, especially mindful of this given his client. He once recalled that when he first met Nike's founder, Knight had announced himself by saying, 'Hi, I'm Phil Knight, and I don't believe in advertising.' But, as Wieden has said, that Knight didn't believe in what they did from the off only gave them licence 'to try things out and do experiments, and a real sense of us against the world. That sort of stupidity led us to do things that caught on, to do the sort of thing people couldn't possibly expect.'

Wieden is said to have been inspired by the final words of murderer Gary Gilmore before his execution by firing squad in 1977 – 'Let's do this', by one account – though, of course, Nike was keen to keep that backstory out of the public conversation. The first suggestion, the even closer 'Let's do it', became the tidier, more imperative 'Just do it' – partly inspired by First Lady Nancy Reagan's mid-1980s 'Just say no' anti-drugs campaign. If it wasn't for that change, Wieden once joked, he would have had to give Gilmore the credit. It was also the more approachable expression of the sentiment that Wieden summarized as 'just go ahead – just fuck it'.

But, it seems, nobody knew what impact the tagline would have. Wieden has said that other creatives at his agency wondered if it was necessary; some

LEFT: A 1980s Nike ad, featuring its famous slogan.

preferred another line that was under consideration – 'Out of Eugene' – that focused on the birthplace of Nike, the running tracks of Eugene, Oregon. An unexcited Nike board thought maybe it could use the 'Just do it' line at some later date. 'Phil Knight said, "We don't need that shit",' Wieden later recalled. 'There were a lot of shrugged shoulders. But [in the end] they let it ride.'

The slogan's first airing, in July 1988, was on a good-humoured commercial – no gung-ho mega sports-star celebrating another championship here – that featured one 'Walt Stack, 80 Years Old', running shirtless for 17 miles as, the ad explains, he does every morning. 'People ask me how I keep my teeth from chattering in the wintertime,' he says as he runs. 'I leave them in my locker.'

And, almost immediately, the tagline appeared to capture the public imagination. It was as though the words formed the go-getting mantra equivalent of a cross-trainer: suitable for multiple uses in life, not just in sports; readily translated into multiple languages, even being published in braille on one poster; vague enough to be interpreted in many ways; positioning Nike – the world's biggest sports marketer, a global corporation – as somehow still being the outsider or the rebel.

'It was the most amazing thing. For some reason that line resonated deeply in an athletic community and just as deeply with people who had little or no connection to sports,' Wieden has said, recognizing that it also put his agency firmly on the map – it would go on to count other huge brands such as Coca-Cola and Old Spice among its clients.

The line was particularly effective for Nike in speaking to women, seeming to be read as an expression of female empowerment. 'If you let me play sports . . . I will like myself more . . . I will have more self-confidence . . . I will be 60 per cent less likely to get breast cancer,' said one Nike commercial from 1995. 'I will learn what it means to be strong,' it concludes. 'Just do it.'

BELOW: 'Just do it' ad from the 1990s.

GROUP THERAPY FROM NIKE.
Just do it.

Nike is, of course, the product of many thousands of people – from designers to those who make the shoes and those who sell them, from marketing minds and advertising agencies to star athletes. But among these many, perhaps four stand out in particular and helped make Nike the brand giant it would become.

Phil Knight

Philip Hampson Knight was born in 1938 in Portland, Oregon, the son of a lawyer and later newspaper publisher. The entrepreneurial skills of trying to break out alone were instilled in him young – his father refused him a summer job on the paper he ran (*The Oregonian*) on the premise that Knight should go out and find work for himself. He has described himself as having 'the personality of a runner. It's lonely. There's pain. You're by yourself. You're thinking.'

RIGHT: Phil Knight, co-founder of Nike, on the cover of *Sports Illustrated* in 1993.

How this man turned a tiny sneaker company into the most powerful force in sports

AUGUST 16, 1993 • $2.95 (CAN. $3.95)

Sports Illustrated

Nike Boss Phil Knight

Knight studied at the University of Oregon (where he met Bill Bowerman), then at Stanford Business School, graduating with an MBA in 1962. Many of Knight's fellow Stanford alumni pursued businesses in electronics – the coming computer revolution. Fortunately, that world was, as Knight has said, 'beyond me – when I turn on a switch and a light bulb comes on, it's magic for me.' Besides, it made sense to him to build a business around what he knew and loved, not whatever was current.

Certainly, Knight was willing to follow a hunch, as he did when he suspected that Japanese-made sneakers were going to outclass – and under-price – those made in Germany, long considered the benchmark. His father thought that was not a good idea. And his father was not alone. 'I've had a lot of people tell me "We think he's not going to make it"', he once observed. 'It was a crazy idea to the outside world, but it never really was to me. We knew we could fail. We just didn't think we would.' By 1993, *The Sporting News* named Knight – rather than any athlete or team owner – 'the most powerful person in sports'.

Perhaps it is this spirit that makes Knight, by his own admission, intensely competitive. At times, he has described his 'contempt' for rival Adidas as 'unhealthy – I despised them'. When, during the 1990s, he was asked if he wanted to meet the president of Reebok, he said no. 'I said I don't know him, I don't like him and I don't want to like him,' Knight would recall decades later. 'And I still feel that way about the competition. There are lots [of companies] we compete with. But, believe me, we will compete.'

'Play by the rules, but be ferocious,' as he has also put it, sounding something like a line from a Nike commercial. So imagine Knight's dismay when, in the early 1980s, he found that Bill Dellinger, an old coaching colleague at the University of Oregon – his alma mater, to which he would give many millions of dollars – was outfitting college athletes with Adidas; and worse, working with the Germans to launch a shoe, the surely pointedly named Adidas Oregon.

'Play by the rules, but be ferocious.'

For Knight, this competitiveness isn't just in sports shoes: in 2002 he bought an animation studio, rebranded it as Laika – a name as similarly short and snappy as Nike's, named after the dog sent into space by the Soviets – and has since gone on to create hit films such as *Coraline* (2009) and *ParaNorman* (2012), the latter of which would be the subject of an Air Foamposite collaboration that same year.

'Nike's culture is young and irreverent – and I'm neither,' Knight once joked. 'The culture is sort of like an individual's personality: you don't get to decide what it is going to be. Nike's culture is not the same as me. [But] I've always said that a businessman can be an artist, just like a painter or a writer or a musician. My work of art is Nike, so I'm devoted to helping it succeed in any way I can.' That, he has said, explains why he retired as chairman in 2016 but continued to be involved.

Now when he sees someone walking down the street in a pair of Nike shoes – which must happen a lot – he says, 'It's still a thrill to this day. It never gets old.' He's unlikely to be recognized: relative to the reach of his brand, Knight remains anonymous, and he has described himself as shy. Not that people would recognize a fellow sneakerhead either: Knight has said that he only owns around 50 pairs of Nike shoes – 'I have a very small closet' – and that a few of those are repeats. 'I don't have all of [Nike's styles] that's for sure,' he told CNBC in 2016. 'I only have two feet.'

Bill Bowerman

Like so many of the names behind Nike, Bill Bowerman was an outstanding college athlete, initially in American football and then track and field. Indeed, after serving in the US Army during the Second World War – during which he was awarded the Silver Star – Bowerman returned to his alma mater, the University of Oregon, to become head coach of the track team.

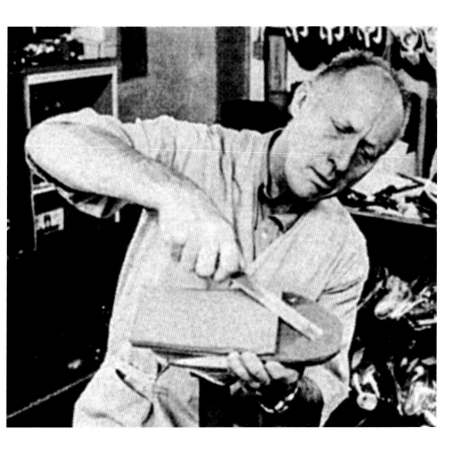

ABOVE: Bill Bowerman, co-founder of Nike.

It was a position that led to huge success – he trained 31 Olympians, including the long-distance runner and future Nike ambassador Steve Prefontaine. It also cemented a lifelong fascination with the science of running, and how it might be improved through the right equipment. He would write frequently to manufacturers of running shoes to explain how the shoes could be improved.

Bowerman would also write to one Adolf Dassler, complimenting him on the quality of his shoes but questioning the sales methods of his representative in the US. Adolf was better known as Adi, founder of a brand called Adidas.

Bowerman's suggestions tended to fall on deaf ears. This only encouraged him to make the improvements himself. He experimented with different leathers for the uppers – including kangaroo leather, deer hide and even snakeskin – and with different materials for the running spikes. He believed the shoe should be tailored to the individual athlete's way of running as much as possible. Among the runners who got to try a pair of Bowerman's homemade shoes were the Olympic track star Otis Davis and a student by the name of Phil Knight. A 50:50 collaboration with Knight would lead to the founding of Blue Ribbon Sports in 1964 and, later, of Nike in 1971. 'If there was no Bowerman, there would be no me,' Knight has said. Always a tactician, Bowerman would later insist that Knight take the larger share of Nike – split 51:49 – so that effective decision-making would not be impeded.

Bowerman was also the man who, arguably, single-handedly brought the whole idea of jogging – not just seriously, around a track, but on the streets, for fun and exercise – to the US, after being introduced the idea of running for fun during a trip to New Zealand in 1962. 'Jogging is a bit more than a walk,' Bowerman wrote for an article published in Portland. 'Start with a short distance then increase as you improve. Jog until you are puffing, then walk until your breathing is normal again. Repeat until you have covered a mile or two, or three.'

Bowerman, arguably, single-handedly brought the whole idea of jogging . . . to the US.

In 1963 Bowerman published a pamphlet, *A Jogger's Manual*, and in 1966 (the year after Blue Ribbon Sports opened its first shop) a complete book on the subject: *Jogging – A Physical Fitness Program for All Ages*. The book, its cover promised, offered (perhaps strangely, given Nike's later emphasis on self-fulfillment through sport and competition) primarily to make its readers look better. It was, 'A medically approved program that will reduce the waistline, improve your appearance, help prolong your life . . . prepared by a heart specialist and a famous track coach, William J. Bowerman.' The book sold over a million copies, a testament to how quickly what was considered a rather esoteric, if not downright odd, activity would soon become a global phenomenon.

Of course, Bowerman – who thought of himself as less a coach so much as a 'professor of competitive response,' as he would describe it – would also be

Bowerman must have asked himself why he wasn't putting these ideas into his own shoes.

ABOVE: The Corsair, made by Onitsuka Tiger.

there with his Onitsuka Tiger and Nike running shoes to capitalize on the fitness trend he was promoting. But to say this was all he was doing would be misleading: Bowerman continued to be a genuine innovator in exploring how running shoes could be better engineered. With every new Onitsuka Tiger model that Blue Ribbon Sports received, Bowerman would literally pick a pair apart to see how it was made – and how it might be improved on, by, for example, adding cushioning or making the shoe lighter.

He would report these ideas back to the Japanese company, which would incorporate them into its later designs, no doubt thankful for the free input. This would be something of a source of conflict between supplier and importer, and no wonder,

given Bowerman's go-getting attitude. As Knight would describe Bowerman's approach to track races in *Shoe Dog*, 'His strategy for running the mile was to start out and run the first two laps at a very fast pace, run the third lap as fast as you can, and on the fourth lap triple your speed.'

When, in 1965, one of Bowerman's University of Oregon runners, Kenny Moore, was recovering from a gash caused by a fellow-runner's spikes, he trained in a pair of Onitsuka Tiger's Tiger TG-22 shoes – a high-jump shoe that Blue Ribbon Sports sold as a running shoe. When Moore developed a stress fracture, Bowerman took a closer look at the shoe's design, discovering that it had no arch support. Designing a shoe that did have this support – it would be unthinkable for any running shoe not to

ABOVE: The Cortez, made by Nike.

have this now – was one of Bowerman's first major innovations, albeit one that Onitsuka Tiger profited from.

It was no wonder, then, that Bowerman must have asked himself why he wasn't putting these ideas into his own shoes, which, of course, he soon did. In 1968 Blue Ribbon Sports released the Corsair, designed by Bowerman but made by Onitsuka Tiger. This was a long-distance running shoe designed to be spikeless, with a full-length midsole and, following Moore's experience, a raised heel to minimize Achilles tendon strain. Sales of the Corsair raked in US$300,000 for the company by the end of the following year, giving it the capital to go fully independent with its own products. Therefore, arguably, it was not clever marketing (giving away pairs of its shoes and a branded t-shirt to any athlete who presented themselves at its first store and could prove they were taking part in the American Olympic trials being held in Eugene) that gave Blue Ribbon Sports the boost it needed to go it alone as Nike; rather, it was clever design.

Bowerman's Corsair design would prove to be the spark of legal wrangles between Onitsuka Tiger and the fledgling Nike, resulting in the style being offered by both companies (see page 122). In 1972, the year that Blue Ribbon Sports' contract with Onitsuka Tiger finally expired, Nike would announce its arrival at the Munich Olympics (where Bowerman was head coach to the US track and field team) with the Cortez, essentially the Corsair but with a different name and Nike branding. However, the success of the Nike Waffle in 1974 (see page 13) only underscored the winning ethos of designing primarily for improved sport performance.

Bowerman's cushioned midsole would, in time, also win him his first patent. This would be the first of eight in total, including those for a cushioned spike plate and a straight last, but also for an external heel counter (a familiar design detail on many high-end training shoes today) and cleated shoes for artificial turf (again, now a sports equipment staple).

With some sad irony, it was experimenting with solvents in a poorly ventilated space that caused Bowerman to suffer nerve damage to his lower legs, leaving him with mobility problems for the rest of his life. He died in 1999, aged 88. Nike's headquarters is now located on Bowerman Drive.

Tinker Hatfield

'I have never really gotten tired of designing new sneakers,' Tinker Hatfield once said. That's just as well, because while Hatfield may have trained as an architect, and has designed electric motorcycles, beer bottles and digital art, he is best known as, arguably, the most influential footwear designer in Nike's story. Like many designers, he thinks of himself first and foremost as a problem solver and believes that 'what really makes sneakers cool are the stories around why they work for an athlete'.

That approach has seen Hatfield design, or have a key part in designing, some of Nike's most pioneering and lasting designs: to name just a few, these include the Air Max 1 (see pages 149–151), Air Safari, Air Sock, Air Jordan 3 (the first to feature the Jumpman logo) and then every Jordan through to the Air Jordan 15 (see pages 151–155). Small wonder, then, that he was once dubbed 'the Michael Jordan of designing Jordans'. Or that Hatfield has received the honour of having a Nike shoe carry his name: the Nike React Tinker Hatfield of 2019.

Hatfield didn't join Nike as a designer, though. His introduction came as a semi-professional college athlete and champion pole-vaulter at the University of Oregon, where he was coached by Bowerman. Hatfield was first hired by Nike in 1981 to illustrate a marketing book. He then designed retail spaces for the company before finally joining the footwear design team in 1984, as one of about nine.

As with Bowerman and Knight's original emphasis on the purpose of Nike, at that time the team's drive was to make the best running shoes, and most people on the design team were runners first, rather than trained in design. As a result, the approach was 'somewhat utilitarian', as Hatfield has noted. 'There

wasn't much focus on aesthetics.' Neither was there a design language that expressed the personality of individual superstar athletes.

ABOVE: Tinker Hatfield, influential footwear designer.

Hatfield would change all of that, initially with a series of deliberately disruptive designs, some of which had to be proven in the field in order to convince Nike to go into large-scale production. For example, the Air Huarache, designed with Eric Avar and launched in 1991 (see pages 136–138), is a shoe that uses neoprene. Just 5,000 pairs were made and taken to the New York Marathon; all sold out in three days and 500,000 pairs were sold the following year. When Michael Jordan requested that Nike use patent leather on a shoe (typically avoided due to it being so thin and pliable), it was Hatfield who found a way to use it as a means of reinforcing the stress points on a basketball shoe.

The timing of Hatfield's vision was important, too: arguably, Nike's emphasis on function at the expense of style – rather than trying to have both – meant its supremacy over the competition was slipping. Hatfield corrected that. 'As a designer you have to pay attention to everything, to observe changes . . . think about them and respond to them,' he said in a 2013 interview with *designboom*. But he has also added a word of warning: 'Good design is appropriate for its time and place. So I can think of many projects that are just too ahead of their time. They haven't become classics because they were

FROM LEFT: Air Jordan 6, Air Jordan 13, Air Safari, Air Huarache, Air Max 1

just too weird. If [people] don't understand it, they might not like it.'

It was Hatfield who could claim to have invented the cross trainer with the Nike Air Trainer 1 (see pages 128–131). Hatfield who came up with the idea of a window on to a pocket of cushioning air – a means of selling the technology by simply showing it – that in 1987 became the Air series (see pages 76–80). He also first proposed self-lacing sneakers; initially as a science-fiction design for *Back to the Future Part II* (1989), but then helping to make them a reality years later with Nike's Hyperadapt 1.0 shoes (see pages 86–89). 'I thought about how a shoe might have an artificial intelligence that could recognize you and then shape to your foot,' Hatfield told *GQ* in 2022. 'I storyboarded the scene where [Marty McFly] puts on the shoes and says "Power laces? All right!"' Hatfield would also design the 'bat boots' for Michael Keaton in *Batman* (1989) and *Batman Returns* (1992).

Yet, for such a forward-thinker, surprisingly Hatfield has said that he didn't see modern sneaker culture coming. 'I don't really understand why everybody is so crazy over sneakers,' he told *Dime* in 2021, 'because I come from an era when everybody just wore [a pair of] Converse.' All the same, he once noted that he sees Nike shoes as 'unique and uniquely American contributions to contemporary design'. What he understood was 'how to go beyond equipment to design in romance and imagery and all of those subliminal characteristics that make an object important to people in less utilitarian ways'.

Michael Jordan

It was the most lucrative endorsement in the history of sports and was certainly the most expensive one for Nike. But what a goldmine it would prove to be, creating in time a sub-brand with almost the reach of Nike itself. It was, as Knight would note, 'the best decision I've ever made in my life'.

In 1984 basketball legend Michael Jordan was just a rookie, yet to play his first season as a professional. But Nike's marketing consultant Sonny Vaccaro saw

LEFT: Hatfield designed the 'bat boots' for Michael Keaton in *Batman* (1989).

something in the young player. Vaccaro was a former PE teacher, an enthusiastic gambler on sporting events and the man who, controversially, pioneered the idea of paying college coaches to kit their players out in Nike shoes (see page 22). He was convinced it was worth betting everything to sign Jordan up to wear Nike shoes, even if that meant his job would likely be on the line.

It was a tough sell. Not only was Jordan an unknown quantity who had never worn Nike shoes, but also, Vaccaro was proposing to offer Jordan twice Nike's annual sponsorship budget for three or four players. And Nike was more associated with unglamorous track-and-field than basketball; Knight was said to even be considering closing the basketball department. On top of this, Nike had just reported its first ever quarterly loss.

Small wonder, then, that another rising star of basketball, Magic Johnson, had rejected Nike's advances once it became clear it couldn't, or wouldn't, pay what he was asking. Nike offered him a sizeable package of shares – a package which, unbeknown to everyone then, would

RIGHT: Michael Jordan playing for the Chicago Bulls in 1991.

have amounted to a fortune in years to come. Johnson, instead, signed with Converse for just US$100,000.

It's little surprise that Jordan said he was unfamiliar with Nike and wanted to sign with either Converse (already home to basketball legend Larry Bird and now to Johnson, too) or Adidas, whose shoes he already wore for practice. But Adidas failed to present him with a contract, and Converse's offer was, just like Johnson's, unremarkable.

Team USA coach George Raveling, Nike's NBA promotions executive Howard White and Jordan's mother, Deloris, helped smooth the way with the player and shape Nike's deal. It wasn't just the money that swayed Jordan, though that must have helped: Nike offered him US$500,000 a year for five years. It didn't, however, throw in the red Mercedes 380SL that Jordan, then just 21, had insisted on from any interested party. Instead, Nike rolled two die-cast models of Mercedes across the boardroom table during negotiations. 'With the money you're going to make, you can buy lots of cars,' Vaccaro told Jordan.

What Jordan did get was the opportunity not to just be seen wearing Nike shoes, but also to have his own pair of shoes made, customized to his specific requests. 'Nobody had taken a player, created shoes and apparel that tied to his style, then launched it all

[at] once,' Nike's then creative director and footwear designer (and later president of Adidas) Peter Moore has said. That wasn't all that was new: it was Deloris's idea for Jordan to get an initial 5 per cent share of profits from the sneakers named after him. He could not have known then how well this groundbreaking sports marketing deal would pay out: Jordan is said to receive at least $150 million in royalties every year.

The first Jordan shoe was released to the public in April 1985. It would be the beginnings of a Jordan brand that would, by 2022, be worth US$5 billion, accounting for over a tenth of all of Nike's sales.

Certainly, the Jordan deal was an unexpectedly major payday for Nike, too. The company, which at first only launched the shoe in six US states, had expected to sell around 100,000 pairs in the first year. Instead it sold 450,000 pairs and generated well over US$100 million in revenue. 'I am the saviour of Nike,' Vaccaro once joked. Later he added: 'No one in the world could have imagined what the Air Jordan would become. Even I never believed that would happen, because nobody had ever done what Nike did.'

By the same token, arguably it was the Brand Jordan phenomenon – buoyed along by Jordan's phenomenal career, leading the Chicago Bulls to six NBA championships and him being named the

NBA's most valuable player five times – that inspired an outright obsession with sneakers.

This was an obsession that, on occasion, took on a literally deadly force. People were robbed of the Jordans on their feet, while in May 1989 a Maryland teenager was found strangled; police theorized that the motive of the victim's 17-year-old killer was to steal his Air Jordans. 'Your Sneakers or Your Life', as the headline in *Sports Illustrated* had it, blaming the sportswear brands, Nike included, for using 'multi-million-dollar advertising campaigns, superstar spokesmen and over-designed, high-price products aimed at impressionable young people [to] create status from the air to feed those who are starving for self-esteem.'

Jordan resonated in positive ways, too: 'Sports is at the heart of American culture, so a lot of emotion already exists around it,' Knight told the *Harvard Business Review* in 1992. 'Emotions are always hard to explain, but there's something inspirational about watching athletes push the limits of performance. You can't explain much in [a commercial that lasts] 60 seconds, but when you show Michael Jordan, you don't have to.'

Remarkably, the Jordan Brand – created in 1997 and including the footwear – was still generating US$2.8 billion in sales for Nike in 2018. That's 15 years after Jordan's retirement from basketball. And in April

2023 a pair of Jordan's 'game-worn' Air Jordan 13s from 1997 sold for US$2.2 million at auction, setting a new world record for the most valuable sneakers ever sold (at the time of writing). The previous record, set in 2021, was also for a pair of Jordans. And the record before that, dating to 2020? For another pair of Jordans.

As for the competition? In 2003 Nike acquired a bankrupt Converse.

BELOW: Nike Air Jordans on the basketball court.

For all that Nike sneakers may be worn by most fans as a style statement, albeit a comfortable one, it's technology – even a kitchen-table, do-it-yourself kind of technology – that is the foundation stone of the company. Picture, for example, co-founder Bill Bowerman pouring a rubber composite into his waffle-maker because he noticed that its indentations – reversed out making small protruding squares – might make for a more springy, all-surfaces alternative to running spikes. The result? The ability to give one of Nike's earliest sneakers a new kind of ethylene vinyl acetate (EVA) sole and the better traction that went with it. Certainly, Nike shoes may so often be chosen for their looks – which is one reason why the brand produces hundreds of styles every year – but Nike's design of sneakers has long foregrounded technological developments in order to improve their functionality.

And, although not as well known for its advancements in clothing textiles, Nike has also developed the likes of its 1991 polyester microfibre

RIGHT: Technology is at the heart of Nike's design.

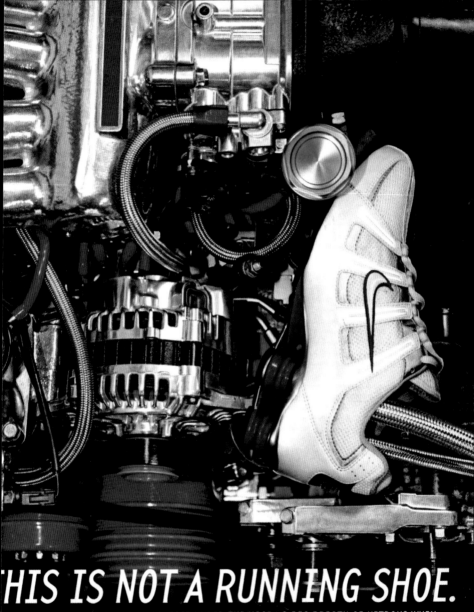

HIS IS NOT A RUNNING SHOE.

IS IS A SUPER-TUNED BLAST OF GO-FAST UNDER THE HOOD, A BIG BREATH OF NITROUS WHEN
U NEED IT, WITH PURE NIKE SHOX RESPONSIVE CUSHIONING TECHNOLOGY TO HARNESS EVERY
T BIT OF HORSEPOWER. SO BE READY WHEN YOU PUT YOUR FOOT TO THE FLOOR. THE NIKE SHOX
RBO AND OTHER TOOLS FOR BETTER RUNNING AT NIKERUNNING.COM.

RUN

fabric Dri-FIT, and, in 2022, Forward, a patented material created by generating fibres from recycled plastic flakes attached using needle-punching machines.

Nike Air

In 1977, when Franklin Rudy proposed his idea for how to make a new generation of Nike shoes bouncier, more springy and more cushioned, it gave sneaker design an entirely new, more hi-tech direction. Perhaps unsurprisingly, Rudy was a former aerospace engineer. What's more, he had first taken the idea to Adidas, who turned it down.

The idea was to build air pockets – more precisely, gas-filled urethane pouches – directly into the sole unit, so that the impact of the foot on the ground wasn't just absorbed through a solid material, however springy it might be; the air pressure in these pockets would, in a sense, push back. More importantly, these pouches wouldn't lose this resistance over time, as foam did. (The pouches were manufactured by a Missouri-based firm called Tetra Plastics, one of the very few companies Nike would acquire, in 1991.) The first shoe to incorporate this 'Air' technology, as Nike would dub it, was the Tailwind, launched in 1979.

It was an immediate hit. Runners who chose the Tailwind had only their experience to go on, but in the following decade, studies by the University of

Tennessee concluded that athletes wearing the shoe expended less energy relative to the more conventional running shoes of the time. With each foot strike the air pockets pushed back, giving the runner propulsion. This was the germination of an idea that, many years later, would prove controversial in top-flight athletics (see React, pages 90–91).

But it took an outside perspective to see the marketing and style potential in what the engineer had devised. The Tailwind had the technology in-built. It was colourful and bold. But, ostensibly, it looked like a conventional running shoe. Designer Tinker Hatfield realized that making the tech visible would make all the difference.

The Tailwind 92 – launched in 1992 – did just that. But, more ostensibly, the Air Max 1, launched on 26 March, 1987, together with the Air Sock, Air Revolution, Air Safari and Air Trainer 1, turned the idea into a whole new, lucrative franchise. Hatfield was, as the man behind visible air, riding what he described as a shift towards 'a looser, street-based, more inspirational form [of design]. I just happened to be doing it from a footwear perspective when nobody else was. There was a bigger appetite for trying something new.'

Hatfield was, he explained, particularly inspired by Norman Foster's Centre Georges Pompidou in Paris.

The architect's radical design innovation was to place all the building's utilities – the electrical boxing, plumbing, air ducts and so on – which were usually hidden, on the outside, for all to see. The logic of doing the same for a technical shoe followed.

The idea did not go unquestioned within Nike. Some argued that it was going too far; that consumers would worry that the pouches looked like they might pop. Yes, it was a gamble. But the company's director of cushioning innovation, David Forland, backed it all the way into production and proved it to be a gamble that paid off. It would mark the creation of a product line that, from that moment on, remained core to Nike's shoe offer, with various iterations – from the Air Max 90 to the Air VaporMax, many of them also designed by Hatfield – along the way.

Nike did not miss the opportunity to drive the idea home. Tinker Hatfield's Air Max BW of 1991 (BW stood for 'Big Window') expanded the visibility of the air pocket right across the sole, giving, as the name suggests, a bigger window on to it. The Air Max 93, meanwhile, went a step further by wrapping the window right around the heel. Then the Air Max 95, designed by Sergio Lozano, introduced two windows to the fore part of the sole, as well as that in the heel. Inevitably, the Air Max 360, introduced in 2006, came with a visible air unit throughout the entire

length of the sole, making it the first shoe to completely replace the use of any foam in the midsole.

Again, the idea evolved further with the Air VaporMax, in which the upper is directly fused onto the sole's multi-chamber air bag, so there's no foam in either the sole or midsole. When Nike ran out of ways of making the air pockets more visible, it turned to making them bigger: the Air Max 2090, launched in 2022, came with an air unit containing 200 per cent more gas than previous examples.

In other words, each iteration of the Air series became ever more technical, and ever readier to express that engineering outwardly, all in the service of increased cushioning. That worked on the track. But it also worked on the street. Nike was by this point not so naive as to be unaware that it was defining and then refining an aesthetic. Yes, Hatfield once noted, 'our primary customer is the athlete. But we also know the bulk of our sales come from people looking for comfort and fashion. It's like the car that goes at 150mph. No one drives at that speed. But it's the coolest cars that go fast.'

It was defining and then refining an aesthetic.

Flyknit

Nike's designers constantly looked for inspiration outside of the shoe world. Tinker Hatfield was a great exponent of travel, noting, for example, how an exhibition on ancient African basket weaving would lead to a basket weave-style upper on shoes such as the Air Footscape, Free Inneva Woven 2 or ACG Watercat.

Unveiled for the 2012 Olympic Games in London, the Nike Flyknit Racer was the first running shoe to be knitted from a high-tensile yarn, allowing it to weigh in at just 160g (5½oz). Sure, it had taken the best part of a decade for Nike to develop, such that by 2015 its

RIGHT: Nike Air More Uptempo, with a full-length Air unit on the sole.

FIT TO *fly*

NIKE FREE FLYKNIT

THE NEW NIKE FREE FLYKNIT
COMBINES THE REVOLUTIONARY
SECOND-SKIN FIT OF FLYKNIT
WITH THE ULTIMATE FLEXIBILITY
OF NIKE FREE FOR A MORE
SUPER NATURAL RIDE.

NIKE.COM/FREEFLYKNIT

ongoing development had seen Nike file some 500
Flyknit-related patents. But the result had much in
its favour: it was not only lighter than leather (by
60g/2oz on average), but more breathable, more
flexible and more form-fitting than leather –
moulding immediately to the wearer's foot, and
doing so without seams that might rub, too.

Indeed, the steps towards the invention of Flyknit are
clear. Nike was always clear on its desire to find a
material that allowed a shoe to wear and feel more
like a sock, without sacrificing the stability and
support of a traditional shoe. This was akin to the
Sock Racer through which Nike had experimented
with textiles back in the late 1980s, much as
Bowerman had experimented with nylon uppers
back in the 1970s.

Such textiles provided the lightness, but not always
the necessary structure. This was a problem that,
in part, led to developments such as 1991's Air
Huarache, with its upper made of neoprene. It
would also lead to the creation of the futuristic Nike
Air Kukini in 1999, designed by Sean McDowell (who
would also design the Air Max Plus and Mayfly
shoes), essentially an attempt to minimize the upper
by use of a stretchy material overlaid with a
scaffolding of rubber struts.

LEFT: Ad for Flyknit from the 2010s.

If the Kukini's functionality was more of a stepping stone than something fully realized, the shoe was nonetheless a big hit in Japan, where its sci-fi aesthetic was appreciated – even leading to a collaboration with Comme des Garçons alumnus Junya Watanabe. The Kukini would be followed the next year by the Air Presto, with its upper made of a medical-industry material called 'space mesh'.

Then, in 2008, Nike unveiled its Flywire technology, which made use of high-strength, lightweight threads as a form of supportive cabling exactly where the support of the foot was needed – much as steel cables are used on a suspension bridge. Further engineering, both micro (this development was very much the product of computer-aided physics and chemistry) and mechanical (including the re-engineering of sock-knitting machines so they could now make shoe uppers) led to Flyknit. With it came its groundbreaking ability to provide the right level of support in all the right places, stretching just so in some directions, but not in others.

Fit was not the only benefit that Flyknit's single-piece upper provided, as vital to athletic performance as this was. It also allowed more creative expression through colour, print and texture than leather. This made it a boon to collaborations with designers, such as Hiroshi Fujiwara on his Nike HTM line from 2002, and blurred the line between performance and style – all the more so when American rapper Kanye West started wearing a pair of Flyknits in 2012.

More than that, Flyknit was a major step in reducing waste relative to the manufacture of cut-and-sewn footwear (comparatively, some 60 per cent less wasteful), especially after Nike later switched to using a recycled polyester yarn. This was important to a company that had faced criticism for its manufacturing policies (see pages 22–24).

Flyknit allowed more creative expression through colour, print and texture than leather.

Flyknit was such a good idea it is little wonder that Nike used it across various sports categories – in shoes for American football, soccer, tennis and golf.

It is also unsurprising that the invention started something of a race for other proprietary knitted-upper technologies. Adidas soon followed suit with its own Primeknit product; and Nike soon followed that with taking the German company to court for copyright infringement, a case that was ultimately dismissed. Nike would sue Skechers, too. After all, Nike is understandably very protective of its idea, given its stated belief that knitted-upper technology is not only set to be the future for Nike, but, ultimately, for the entire sports-shoe industry.

The Self-Lacing Shoe

Perhaps the most futuristic of all of Nike's innovations is the self-lacing shoe. This was an idea that Tinker Hatfield proposed in his design of the then fictional Nike MAG (named for the magnetic levitation of Marty McFly's hoverboard) for *Back to the Future Part II* (1989). However, the designer always saw the practical potential of the idea were it ever to be realized. It would allow basketball players to loosen their shoes in the gaps between play, for example, then have their shoes tighten quickly when play began; it would have advantages for the immobile, who couldn't easily reach down to fasten their footwear; and, of course, it would be a boon to the lazy, as well as tie in with the street style of wearing sneakers with laces untied for easy pull-on and slide-off.

Few, however, might have imagined back in 1989 that self-lacing shoes would be anything more than a fun idea. But when, in 2015, a one-off pair of shoes by the name of Adapt BB was auctioned for the Michael J. Fox Foundation, it seemed to offer the real thing. The pair had what Nike called E.A.R.L., or Electro Adaptive Reactive Lacing.

Remarkably, embedded in the shoes, and controlled by a button on their side or by app, was a tiny motor

RIGHT: Michael J. Fox wearing the fictional Nike MAG in *Back to the Future Part II.*

connected to a series of equally tiny cables that would then loosen or tighten according to the wearer's need. Nike would follow up with a second generation of the shoe for public sale and then installed the tech in basketball sneakers, too.

Lunarlon

The Lunarlon sole, developed by designers Eric Avra and Kevin Hoffer, was – as the name suggests – inspired by film of astronauts walking, or, more accurately, bouncing over the Moon's surface in low gravity. The two designers wanted a system that would protect the foot from the impact of the 40,000 or so steps that a marathon runner takes from start to finish, or that would likewise provide a cushion for basketball players after their jumps – and maybe give them a more explosive spring for the way up, too. The sports shoe industry's standard cushioning material was ethylene vinyl acetate (EVA), first used by Bowerman on the 1974 Nike Waffle Racer.

Appropriately enough, after trialling countless super-light yet super-bouncy materials and drawing a blank, Nike uncovered a foam-like material – a blend of EVA and nitrite rubber – developed by its Advanced Material Interest Group years before but finding no home at the time. That was, perhaps, because while it was around 30 per cent lighter than EVA, it was also 'as sticky as melted marshmallows', as Hoffer once put it.

It took yet more countless experiments – including freezing the material in the Nike Innovation Kitchen – before Nike came up with a proprietary, stable material that could be squeezed into an EVA foam shell (which Nike calls Phylon) that held it all in place, heat-expanding it and then cooling it in a mould. Ridges, running lengthways along the sole, were then added to allow it to compress more than it otherwise would.

These shoes had . . . a 'running-on-pillows feel' . . . without additional weight or bulk

After a prototype was made in 2005, the first official shoes to carry the technology, released in 2008, were the Lunaracer (for those marathon runners) and the Hyperdunk (for the ballers). These shoes had what Hoffer described as a 'running-on-pillows feel' but, crucially, provided this without additional weight or bulk and, just as importantly, with durability. If foam soles inevitably 'bottomed out' all too quickly, losing their bounce-back as the tiny bubbles within the material pop and stay compressed, this degradation process was greatly extended by Lunarlon. Avra and Hoffer could immediately see its potential for other applications, notably on skateboard shoes, the likes of the SB Eric Koston 1 (1997), and snowboard shoes, the likes of the LunarENDOR (2014).

React

Of course, Nike did not stop there. It knew that Lunarlon, while a giant leap for sporting kind, was not perfect. In 2017 came another advance in sole technology called React, which the company would claim eliminated or greatly improved the compromises required with Lunarlon: the 'compression over time' issue faced by all foams; that it had to be encased in a firmer protective carrier that, inevitably, limited the responsiveness of the foam inside; and the fact that putting the foam inside the carrier meant gluing two densities of foam together, which was complex and fiddly.

React, in contrast, was all one piece and didn't use EVA at all, instead employing a thermoplastic elastomer (TPE) base and using computer analysis to precisely vary the React cushioning in different areas of the sole for maximum benefit to the runner. React, Nike claimed, was 11 per cent softer but offered 13 per cent more 'energy return' relative to Lunarlon.

There wasn't actually any return of energy back to the runner – there was no propulsion for the foot as the material filled out back into shape. Rather, while more traditional EVA foam tended to dissipate 40–60 per cent of the force needed to compress them during running, React 'robbed' the runner of much less. React sprung back faster. Surveys the company conducted suggested that it made runners want to run – a Nike nirvana.

But this entire idea would in time prove controversial in some professional sporting circles, raising the question of whether it – and similar technologies from other brands – was no longer merely a running shoe and now more of a running aid. When, in 2019, the Kenyan runner Eliud Kipchoge became the first person to run a marathon distance in under two hours, this incredible human feat was somewhat tarnished by criticism of his shoes, a pair of Nike Vaporfly – the 'energy return' of their React foam soles now further enhanced by a series of carbon-fibre plates embedded within them.

Such was the concern that these were a form of performance enhancement that World Athletics,

BELOW: Ad for React from the 2010s.

SADIE SINK
ACTRESS

INSTANT

NIKE REACT

NIKE.COM/REACT

running's governing body, subsequently banned the shoes from competition, setting new rules on the maximum sole thickness and the number of carbon plates allowed, and mandating that the shoes had to be available for anyone to buy for at least four months before they could be used in a competition.

Nonetheless, React proved a hit for its cushioned but firm ride, first appearing in two basketball shoes – the React Hyperdunk basketball shoe (2017) and the Jordan Super.Fly (2017) – then the React Element 87 running shoe (2019) and many more lifestyle-oriented shoes. Many people, it seemed, liked putting more of a bounce in their step. In China, Nike even launched an immersive experience called Reactland, in which shoppers would run on a treadmill to control an avatar of themselves running through a fantasy landscape that represented the soft, bouncy and lightweight qualities of the shoe.

React wasn't the last of Nike's endeavours to cushion the foot. Another system, ZoomX (launched in 2016), was made using the lightweight polymer Pebax. Joyride, launched in 2019, used thousands of TPE beads strategically placed in pods along the sole, allowing the foam to expand in all directions, and creating a more personalized footbed.

Is all of this scientific cleverness lost to many Nike fans? For some of them, it's the old, now technologically dated, classic styles that still resonate the most. But for the company itself, it's the new, technically more advanced ones that move the sneaker conversation on.

Such was the concern that these shoes were a form of performance enhancement that World Athletics banned them.

Certainly, that has led to some curiosities: take, for example, the likes of the similarly adaptive GO FlyEase, launched in 2021. Mechanically, it's a fundamentally different way of looking at athletic shoes and, one might say, of wearing them, too. The FlyEase allows someone to put them on and take them off without touching them. How so? Essentially, the shoe is based on a durable elastic band that stretches entirely around it, incorporating a hinge in front of the heel. Step into the shoe and the hinge locks close and the band tightens around your foot. Put one foot on the heel of the other to click open the hinge and the shoe springs open, allowing you to step out. Strange? Maybe now. But it's a testament to Nike's enduring ethos of always thinking ahead.

While Nike makes innovative shoes, loaded with design and engineering content, its significance to popular culture goes far beyond its products. More than many big brands, it has symbolic value – of status, culture, identity – sufficiently resonant that it would become the subject of a film of its own, Ben Affleck's *Air* (2023).

Nike in the Movies

There is a scene in Spike Lee's *Do The Right Thing* (1989) when one of the characters, Buggin' Out, looks down at his sneakers with abject horror. A passer-by pushing a bike has somehow brushed up against them, leaving a scuff mark. These, Buggin' explains to the cyclist, 'were my brand-new white Nike Air Jordans that I just bought'. The man apologizes but clearly doesn't grasp the significance. Buggin's friends weigh in: 'Your Jordans are fucked up!' says one. 'Might as well throw them shits out – they're broke, man!' another tells him. 'How much did you pay for them? US$108 with tax!' 'I should make you buy me another pair!' Buggin' concludes. But the

RIGHT: Buggin' Out not happy about his scuffed shoes in *Do The Right Thing*.

cyclist just doesn't get it: all this fuss over a little mark on a pair of sneakers.

Do the Right Thing isn't the only time that a pair of Nike sneakers has played a starring role in a film. Lee – a lifelong Nike fan who appeared in goofy character in Nike commercials with Michael Jordan – also highlights a pair of Air Foamposite Pros in *He Got Game* (1998), another of his films. There are, of course, the *Space Jam* movies, from 1996 onwards – vehicles for Michael Jordan's star power. And there are the Air Mags designed for *Back to the Future Part II* (1989) and the custom Air Trainer 2s created for *Batman* (1989).

But there are also the Nike Vandals worn by the time-travelling character Kyle Reese in *The Terminator* (1984) and again in *Terminator Genisys* (2015), despite Nike's attempts to convince the costume designer the character should now be wearing a pair of Air Force 1s. Characters Brandon and Chunk wear Vandal Supremes and Terra TCs, respectively, in *The Goonies* (1985), with one pair – customized to release a slippery oil from their heels in order to thwart pursuers – being described punningly as 'slick shoes'. Tom Hanks wears a pair of Air Force 2s to play a giant piano, by jumping on the keys, in *Big* (1988), and a pair of Cortez as the title character of Forrest Gump (1994) – 'Run Forrest, run!' – which posits the eponymous character accidentally starting the craze for jogging.

There are the Air Woven worn by Bill Murray's character in *Lost in Translation* (2003) – the Japanese streetwear designer and collaborator Hiroshi Fujiwara even has a cameo in the film; and the Cortez worn by Leonardo DiCaprio as banker Jordan Belfort in *The Wolf of Wall Street* (2013). *White Men Can't Jump* (1992), inevitably, has multiple Nike shoe styles throughout. In *George of the Jungle* (1997), Brendan Fraser is shipped in a crate back to his African homeland, and bursts outside wearing, what else, but a pair of Air More Uptempo.

ABOVE: Tom Hanks as Forrest Gump with a pair of Cortez.

Naturally, given Nike's growing prowess in marketing throughout the 1980s and beyond, the company would become a master of product placement, some instances making more sense to the narrative than others. But, in many instances, the presence of a pair of Nike shoes was more the director or costume designer's choice – Nike was just felt to be the most relevant option. In part, this is down simply to the fact that while other brands certainly made competent sports shoes, they did not carry the same cultural cool as Nike.

The Non-Conformist

Nike has nurtured its image as an agitator or insurgent against the norms of the times. Although a global business (valued in excess of US$100 billion and so very much locked into capitalistic power structures, as sociologists might see things), as well as being a company that has not been fearful of using its muscle to push for terms and political candidates that better suited its business, Nike's public face has reflected its ability to finesse its reputation for bucking norms through non-conformism.

In its encouragement of the broad swathe of socially excluded groups, Nike has thought outside of the mainstream. That might mean designing, for

RIGHT: Basketball superstar, Sheryl Swoopes.

ABOVE: A Nike hijab, observing the needs of Muslim athletes.

example, the first basketball shoe specifically for women and the first sports shoe to carry a female athlete's name (in the guise of 1995's Air Swoopes, for WNBA superstar Sheryl Swoopes); supporting the idea that girls should play sport (from 1994); through to Nike observing the religious needs of Muslim athletes (from 2017).

Whether it's the politically charged backing of Colin Kaepernick in 2018 in the face of calls for a boycott (see page 25) or its highlighting the likes of Shaquem Griffin, NFL rookie and amputee, through its endorsement of the player the same year, Nike has repeatedly pushed against mainstream acceptable opinion to underscore its rebel image. 'We like a little wackiness,' Knight said to CBS in 2016. 'We just don't want too much.'

This has worked, in part, because, since 2017 at least, Nike has focused its sales towards younger, metropolitan and, above all, urban consumers living in the world's most dynamic and wealthy cities, from New York to LA, London to Berlin, Beijing to Seoul and Tokyo. In other words, Nike has focused its attention on its core demographic – those more likely to find resonance with the company's liberal-leaning stance on 'hot potato' issues of the day.

But, long before this, Nike was ready to explore off-beat ideas: the likes of Andre Agassi playing 'rock 'n' roll' tennis on a stage-cum-court alongside the Red Hot Chili Peppers in 1991, for example, with even the tennis player exiting the scene muttering 'that was weird' to himself; or basketball player Penny Hardaway having a phone conversation with L'il Penny, a small puppet version of himself in 1996; or, in one 2007 commercial for the Brazilian market, a rejection of cosmetic surgery through the medium of hospital gown-wearing dancers.

Nike has been ready to subvert the usual brand-building methodologies in unconventional ways, with even a hint of rebuke to the viewers and potential customers: 'I am not a role model,' as NBA player Charles Barkley intones in a 1993 commercial. 'I am not paid to be a role model. I am paid to wreak havoc on the basketball court. Parents should be role models. Just because I dunk a basketball doesn't mean I should raise your kids.'

McENROE SWEARS BY THEM.

Indeed, Nike's choice of brand ambassadors has been crucial in building this outsider status – 'the underdog culture,' as Knight has called it. While the company has repeatedly signed some of the most expensive, multi-million-dollar endorsement deals with its athletes, these athletes have, arguably, all had some kind of edge to them, in their individualistic attitude as much as their exceptional ability, which sometimes allowed Nike to play a part in that sport's transformation into something modern and voguish; to make it, as Tinker Hatfield has said, 'part of the street culture'.

This was true from the start. As Pat Tyson would say of his former teammate and Nike's first ambassador,

Steve Prefontaine, 'Pre was flashy – he'd drive around in convertible cars wearing a fringed leather coat and flared trousers. He was the guy.' Knight has described Prefontaine as being 'the soul of the company'. Tragically, Prefontaine died when he crashed his MG sportscar into a roadside rock. (His story was told in the 1998 film *Without Limits*, Prefontaine being played by Billy Crudup and Bowerman by Donald Sutherland.) He came to be known as 'the James Dean of Track', and this line perhaps inspired a 1980s poster of Nike's ambassador and tennis player John McEnroe – 'Rebel With a Cause' – that paid homage to Dennis Stock's classic 1955 shot of Dean walking through a rainy New York.

Nike, in fact, had turned to McEnroe in 1978 somewhat by accident, intending to sign Jimmy Connors, who had agreed to wear Nike shoes. However, when Connors seemed to prevaricate about signing a contract, Nike walked away. When Knight went to the next Wimbledon tournament and saw McEnroe erupt at a judge over a line call, he knew he had found the perfect ambassador. 'I became a fan of his intensity and his competitiveness and his attitude,' Knight would say.

'I became a fan of [McEnroe's] intensity and his competitiveness and his attitude.'

ABOVE: American tennis player Andre Agassi at the US Open in 1990.

Nike was lucky – or prescient – in spotting McEnroe's public appeal, as divisive as that could be. When the tennis player hit his ankle and began wearing Nike mid-top shoes – which would become the Air Trainer 1 – to aid recovery, sales leapt from 10,000 pairs per annum to over a million. McEnroe is, to date, the athlete who has been with Nike the longest.

'When people were telling me to back off, the powers that be were telling me they were going to suspend me, [Knight] would be calling me and telling me to keep doing the same thing,' McEnroe would recall. 'Phil was a maverick. Maybe he saw someone who was a kindred spirit. The way Nike used me in commercials was sort of embellishing what I was doing. It took what I was – what appeared to be a negative for some people – and made it a positive. I think that's the way he has operated through the years.'

After McEnroe in 1990 there was Andre Agassi, wearing denim shorts, cropped Spandex tops, bold graphics and neon pink Air Tech Challenge 2 shoes

RIGHT: American tennis champion Serena Williams at the US Open in 2004.

to play Grand Slam tennis – challenging tournament rules much as Michael Jordan had done with his red-and-black basketball boots (see pages 152–154). 'It just started with me being opinionated and Nike having a sense of being willing to push boundaries,' the new 'bad boy of tennis' once explained. 'A lot of it had to do with the rebellious phase I was in, so anything that broke the establishment idea was a big motivator at the time. People felt the freedom to let [tennis] be what it needed to be. I was just a teenager willing to take chances with a company also willing to take chances.'

As Tinker Hatfield would say of him: 'Andre was different – he lived in Vegas, for crying out loud. [And] he was the perfect vehicle for us to turn tennis into a different kind of sport', an idea later echoed by Serena Williams when she signed with Nike in 2003: 'I wanted to make sport and fashion more synonymous.'

Legends

The growing list of Nike's ambassadors reads like a roll-call of yet more sporting legends: in soccer the likes of Neymar Jr – one of the first athletes to create his shoe line in partnership with the Jordan brand; in golf the likes of Rory McIlroy and Tiger Woods – Woods parting company with Nike in 2024 after an incredible 27-year run; in baseball Derek Jeter; in basketball Bo 'Bo Knows' Jackson, Kobe Bryant (who finally got to have his own shoe after his retirement) and, of course, Michael Jordan; in tennis Serena Williams, Maria Sharapova and Rafael Nadal.

Nike has had an open mind about endorsement deals, too, sometimes continuing to support its athletes even when they are facing a storm of bad publicity. It renewed its contract with Tiger Woods despite the media furore surrounding his infidelities, for example. Cheating in sport was another matter. In 2012 Nike declined to renew its long-standing agreement with the cyclist Lance Armstrong. Similarly, in 2018 it did not renew with Sharapova after she admitted to failing a doping test in 2018 (Nike had signed with her when she was just 11 and she had, at one point, the most expensive deal ever signed with a female athlete); it was later ruled that the doping was unintentional.

ABOVE: Kobe Bryant in a Nike ad in 2010.

More embarrassingly, Nike had to weather the fall from grace of Alberto Salazar – long-time Nike training guru and head coach of the Nike Oregon Project to study the effects of high elevation on athletic performance. In 2019 his coaching accreditation was withdrawn for, it was accused, facilitating doping. The idea of this happening on Nike's home turf, said CEO Mark Parker, 'makes me sick'.

Nike likewise pioneered the idea of signing an athlete not just for a term of so many years but for life, betting on an athlete continuing to have resonance long after their playing days are over. American basketball player LeBron James – lured away from Adidas – and Portugese footballer Cristiano Ronaldo, for example, each took a billion-dollar payday (in 2015 and 2016, respectively) to commit to working with Nike basically forever. If that kind of massive money deal sounds excessive, one report suggested that Ronaldo's high social media presence alone generated almost US$500 million a year for the sports company.

Not that money always talks; Knight has spoken of his regrets at not being first to successfully sign some athletes. While these athletes may gain kudos for their ties with Nike, they are also looking for the best financial package. Argentine footballer Lionel Messi signed young with Nike but left in 2006 for rival Adidas; Nike took Messi to court to try to keep him, but a Spanish judge ruled in the footballer's favour. And in 2018 Swiss tennis legend Roger Federer turned down a sponsorship deal with Nike so he could pursue other, very lucrative options.

Nonetheless, the successful deals helped Nike build a store of credibility – both sporting and in terms of lifestyle appeal – that echoed at the tills and also operated in parallel with pop culture's embrace of the Nike brand.

Collaboration

Nike has been cited many times in hip-hop lyrics and
has proven to be inspiration for entire songs: from
Nelly's 'Air Force Ones' (2002), through to Drake's
'Jumpman' (2015) and Frank Ocean's 'Nikes' (2016).

In 2007 Nike was able to parlay that association
into a collaboration with rapper Kanye West, the
company's first full collaboration with a celebrity
who was not also an athlete and leading to some of
its most collectible models. Among these, infamously,
was the all-red Yeezy 2 style – a.k.a. Red October –
co-designed with Nike creative director Mark Smith.
It was teased ahead of its launch by rapper Jay-Z –
who exclaimed 'shout-out to me Yeezys, Yeezy 2s'
during a performance – and continued to command
high tens of thousands of dollars through reseller
markets long after its 2012 launch.

This was just the first of many such collaborations
that Nike would pursue outside of the sports arena.
The company might be said to have bucked its
formula of signing mega-deals with the mega-stars
of sports by establishing another – collaborating
with well-respected creatives – that could drive
appeal to consumers inspired by more 'highbrow'
street culture, art and fashion.

Among these countless shoe design collaborators
have been not just West but also the likes of the
musicians Drake (2013) and Travis Scott (2017);

the graffiti artists Futura 2000 (2003) and Stash
(2006); and contemporary artists Piet Parra (2005)
and Tom Sachs – who, following his 2012 Mars Yard
shoe, would go on to create a new category of
sneaker for Nike's progressive NikeCraft division
with what he called the General Purpose Shoe.

Design-led collaborations have included streetwear
labels such as Stüssy (2000), Supreme (2002) and
CLOT (2006) – which played a part in propelling this
latter brand to its own stratospheric success. Other
partnerships have included with specific urban
design stores such as the Tokyo sneaker boutique
Atmos (2002) and Jeff Staple's Reed Space in New
York (2005) – helping to make both cities epicentres
for the rarest of Nike shoes. And some collaborations
have just been with leading sneakerheads, the likes
of American DJ Bobbito Garcia.

There have been collaborations with fashion design
heavyweights such as Rei Kawakubo (1999), founder
of Comme Des Garçons; Jun Takahashi (2010),
founder of the cult Japanese brand Undercover and,
with Nike, of the long-standing technical running line
Gyakusou; with Riccardo Tisci (2014), then of
Givenchy; with Virgil Abloh (2017), of Off-White and
Louis Vuitton; with Sean Wotherspoon in 2017; and

LEFT: Kanye West performing at the
Grammy Awards in 2008 wearing a
prototype of the Nike Air Yeezy 1.

with Martine Rose, who in 2019 reinvented the clunky
Air Monarch 4 as something more deliberately clunky
and pink. And there have even been tie-ins with
Apple, Playstation and, in 2020, Ben & Jerry's – giving
rise to the fantastically named Chunky Dunky.

Not all of these collaborations have been entirely
successful. The industrial designer Marc Newson's
Zvezdochka shoe of 2004 – Nike's first entirely
computer-designed model – comprised a bootie-like
sock over which a perforated outer could be pulled
and was designed for use on the International Space
Station; it never made it into space but was
nonetheless hugely influential on the sneaker
design that followed.

And while Stephen Powers, better known as the
contemporary artist ESPO, may have convinced

Nike to make its first transparent shoe, the ESPO
Air Force 2 Low, in 2004 – 'a performance shoe,
but performing as art,' as Powers put it – the sports
company's designers did warn him that actual
performance as footwear might be an issue. 'Within
two blocks the plastic was cutting my feet,' Powers
has recalled. 'I never wore them again.'

ABOVE: The Nike
Chunky Dunky.

But these instances can't really be called failures.
As Nike's former CEO Mark Parker noted, 'outside
collaborations push us towards the edges as a
company – [and] through that exchange, it
accelerates our own culture of thinking and
innovating'. In other words, it helped position
Nike not just as a force of innovation within sports,
but also within the world of design and style.

While functionality was the main concern of Bowerman and Knight's designs for Nike, even from its earliest days they had at least half an eye on style, too. Among its first six shoes was, for example, the Flyte-Wet. This had many attributes that made it better to run in – a 'gum rubber sole, sponge midsole with all-ground foxing, padded ankle cushion,' as an advertisement of the era proclaimed. But it was also the first wet-look shoe, with a 'liquid-looking polyurethane coating [giving] the model a perpetual shine'. This added nothing to the runner's experience. It just looked good.

'When we started out, we had 12 styles of shoe, and three of those were the same model,' Knight once laughed as he toured one of his own stores with Fox News in 2016. 'So it blows me away how many styles we have now – tens of thousands over the years. We've come a long way.'

Nike has proven itself capable of repeatedly rewriting the rules of sneaker design –

RIGHT: Virgil Abloh wearing his Louis Vuitton x Air Force 1.

IRREVERENCE. JUSTIFIED.

Listen up. See that color? It's not just there to make noise. It's where we put Durathane, a revolutionary new material that doubles the toe-piece life. And that's just half of it. The Tech Challenge has full-length Nike-Air cushioning, and Durabuck uppers for repeated machine washing. So go ahead. Be irreverent, make some noise on the court. It's justified.

ABOVE: Ad for Nike Air Tech Challenge.

technologically, yes, but also aesthetically, the latter often growing out of the former. It has meant that the company has developed a broad church of followers, each wedded to their own look for their own reasons – some passionate about more heritage styles, others the more outlandish, futuristic ones. But it has also been the brand behind many of what would come to be regarded as sneaker design classics. Nearly all of them were, in their time, groundbreaking in some way – in their construction or style, in the way they were marketed or in what or who they represented. Inevitably, just a few are considered below.

Air Force 1

The Air Force 1 is one of Nike's most enduring styles, perhaps its definitive shoe. Named after the US president's private airliner, it launched in 1982, complete with Nike's new Air technology.

It was designer Bruce Kilgore's first basketball shoe, even if court shoes would be what he'd become known for (among them the Adversary, Air Ace and Avenger tennis shoes, together with the Air Pressure and Air Jordan 2). Prior to that, he had been busy developing track spikes, notably the Zoom mesh model that helped American athlete Carl Lewis power to multi-gold-winning victory at the 1984 Olympics. And prior to Nike, Kilgore was busy helping to design cars, notably the Pontiac Fiero and boxy Chrysler K-Car, the model said to have saved Chrysler from oblivion. He would go on to co-design the Air Max 180 and design the Air Ships, among other Nike shoes.

The success of the style was by no means certain. This was the first time Nike had used slip-last construction, by which the upper is pulled over the last (the foot-shaped form) and then stitched to the midsole in order to make for a more flexible shoe. Kilgore took samples to US colleges to get basketball players' feelings on whether it would work to play in. It did.

The shoe was a hit with basketball players. Six of the top players at the time, 'the original six',

ABOVE: The Air Force 1.

adopted the Air Force 1 on its release, lending the shoe considerable performance credibility. But it was also a success in street culture, where its clean silhouette, thick sole and essential simplicity would make it ripe for customization and design collaborations. It is maybe the closest shoe Nike has to, say, Converse Chuck Taylors or Adidas Stan Smiths. All this would make it what's believed to be Nike's highest-selling shoe of all time.

Strangely, in retrospect, the Air Force 1 looked to be short-lived. Nike decided to discontinue the model only two years after its release. Nobody is quite clear on why, but perhaps to make way for other benchmark styles, the Air Jordan 1 and Dunk, in the pipeline for 1985. Kilgore had himself moved on, working on what might be considered the first luxury sneaker in the guise of the Air Jordan 2, with its high-quality leathers, 'made in Italy' construction and sartorial lines and brogueing.

But if Nike wasn't sure about it, urban fashion was. When the Air Force 1 was reintroduced in 1986, it was because Nike had been persuaded to do so by landmark Baltimore sneaker retailers Charley Rudo Sports, Cinderella Shoes and Downtown Locker Room. 'If you guys are crazy enough to ask for it, then we're crazy enough to make it for you', Cinderella Shoes' Paul Blinken recalled Nike as saying – though Nike did insist the stores take huge minimum orders. Yet they had to place a new order the following month, requesting a new colour Air Force 1 every month into the deal. Thus the 'Color of the Month' programme was created.

The style became an urban phenomenon, driven not by Nike's marketing might but by pre-internet word of mouth, one kid at a time. It was specifically the model's 'triple white' all-white incarnation that was quickly embraced by the hip-hop scene in New York, especially that revolving around Harlem. Here, sneakers were gaining cultural cachet as status items, notably in a city whose populace does a lot of walking. This won Air Force 1s the nickname of 'uptowns', because you had to go up town to Manhattan to buy a pair.

Even then, the style was worn not just for its looks but for its function – playing streetball on hard concrete was tough on the feet, such that players would often wear multiple pairs of socks for extra cushioning. The Air Force 1's Air technology did away with that need. Some have credited the Air Force 1 as the model that brought sport – basketball specifically – and hip-hop together in a shared aesthetic, one that would go on to become available in more colour variations than any other Nike shoe.

Cortez

The shoe that launched Nike – originally designed by Bowerman and manufactured by Onitsuka Tiger in 1968 (see pages 60–61), and offered in several hundred different versions since – was almost called the Aztec. This idea of Bowerman's was to be a nod to the Meso-Americanas who had inhabited what would become Mexico, and it was just in time for the 1968 Mexico Olympics. The problem? Adidas already had a shoe called the Azteca Gold – and were already lining up their lawyers if Nike didn't change the name of their shoe.

Knight was not happy about this situation, being as competitive as he was, especially when it came to rival sports shoe manufacturers. So when Bowerman asked, 'Who's that guy who kicked the shit out of the Aztecs?' calling the shoe the Cortez – after the 16th-century Spanish explorer and conquistador Hernán Cortés – seemed like the perfect rebuff.

What neither of them could have known was how the style would, arguably, become their icon: simple,

RIGHT: American actress Farrah Fawcett wearing the Cortez.

graphic, affordable, with some innovative details for the time, including a sponge midsole, herringbone-pattern sole and, instead of leather, an upper made from a lightweight nylon resin that the company called 'Swoosh fiber'. One Blue Ribbons Sports advertisement described the Cortez as 'the finest long-distance shoe in the world', adding that 'the Cortez is also ideal for casual wear'.

It would become an icon so fast that, having turned people into, as Knight had it, 'full-blown Cortez addicts,' the company struggled to meet supply. The situation was compounded by the shoe being worn by the rock 'n' roll athlete – and Nike's first sponsored athlete – Steve Prefontaine, at the 1972 Munich Olympics.

But, having tapped the zeitgeist, that demand also made the Cortez a shoe worth fighting for. That's why, in 1971, after a court battle with Onitsuka Tiger, Nike was relieved to win the right to continue making the Cortez, leaving the Japanese maker to continue to make its version, the Corsair. The shoe Nike unveiled in 1972 was more or less the same as the Corsair, though now it carried the Swoosh. Advertising telling 'The Cortez Story' neatly airbrushed Onitsuka Tiger from history.

That wasn't the last of the challenges associated with the Cortez, however. The shoe would, in retrospect, provide an important lesson for Nike –

still a very male company, comprising a bunch of men united by a shared passion for running, at a time when women were still being sidelined in athletics. As such, Nike didn't take all that seriously the business opportunity to sell to women from the outset, and was caught completely off-guard when, five years later, Farrah Fawcett – making her escape on a skateboard – wore a pair of Senorita Cortez in an episode of *Charlie's Angels*, sparking a run on the shoes.

The Cortez would find a life of its own, in some senses beyond Nike's control. While it would be superseded by far more technically advanced running shoes, the style's pop-culture cachet just kept growing, in no small part for being one of Nike's earliest shoes. As Nike built its presence in California (Blue Ribbon Sports opened its first store in Santa Monica), the Cortez would, for example, become one of the few sneakers worn as a staple of Cholo style – the subculture expressing Chicano identity, favouring bandanas, oversized white t-shirts and crisp Dickies trousers.

So strong was this association with what was regarded as a gang culture – the Cortez was said to have been adopted as the official footwear of the LA-based Mara Salvatrucha gang – that students in LA schools would be sent home if they were wearing a pair. The fact that the shoe would become a standard among LA's hip-hop culture, too, with Snoop Dogg and Eazy-E, of NWA, all favouring the style, didn't seem to be an issue. They weren't the only musicians with a feel for the style: during his 1980 world tour, British singer Elton John traded tickets to his shows for US$16,000 worth of Nike shoes, including a batch of blue and white Cortez to go with his baseball-inspired stage costume.

Air Presto

The Air Presto was released in 2000, ahead of the Sydney Olympics that year. One of the most technically advanced shoes developed at that point, it was designed to mimic the freedom felt in running without shoes at all. The Presto was designed by Tobie Hatfield, Tinker Hatfield's brother, at Nike's recently opened research laboratory in Taiwan. There, he was left to his own creative devices, which may explain some of the more unusual aspects of the shoe.

When Nike referred to its new Air Presto running shoe as 'a t-shirt for your feet', it was driving not just at the shoe's lack of weight and barely there comfort, but also that, radically, the shoe came in sizes XXS though to XXXL. This was the result of a happy discovery: Hatfield had arranged for a colleague to be given a prototype pair for trial. And although this size 11 person was, unknowingly, given a size 9, so form-fitting was the shoe that he had no complaints about the fit.

That had been Hatfield's holy grail on this project.
He had recalled a production meeting he'd attended
in Korea in which the group all tried on new styles
– and he hated his for the way the collar splayed
out. That prompted the idea: surely there was some
form or use of materials that made for a sports shoe
that properly hugged the foot and was comfortable.
And if that was possible, maybe, Hatfield thought,
more generic sizing in a shoe would be possible, too.

This, however, was not the most unusual aspect
of the experimental Presto. The shoe was also,
untypically, launched in multiple colours from the off
– 13 in all. All bar one were given off-beat nicknames
such as Migraine Fly, Abdominal Snowman, Shady
Milkman, Rabid Panda and Rogue Kielbasa. Each
was also given its own equally surreal animated TV
commercial, created by Wieden+Kennedy and
featuring monks with balloons for heads, urinating
clouds and, yes, a milkman of dubious intent putting
some unidentified substance in his milk.

ABOVE: The
Air Presto.

Even how the shoe was named was a break with norms: Nike sent an invitation out to the wider design community asking for names for the shoe and received over 300 submissions. One of these suggested 'Presto Magic' – the suggestion being that people could just throw on the shoe and be ready to go, just like that – which Nike reduced to 'Presto'. CEO Mark Parker had wanted to call the shoe the Air Comfy; fortunately, a New England slipper manufacturer already had the legal right to that one, even if Parker, for a moment, considered an acquisition just to get the name.

All this fun, however, belied the fact that the Presto was a product of Nike's late 1990s Alpha Project department, charged with realizing the most progressive ideas in sports shoe design – a fact signified by the five tell-tale dots on the outsole. In many ways, the Presto was a shoe that combined some of the best thinking of previous designs. It had a Phylon midsole and cushioned Duralon outsole. It had a raised toe bumper and a rubberized cage that wrapped supportively around the mid-section of the foot like an exoskeleton; this was said to be inspired by the semi-transparent, colourful casings of Apple's iMac G3 computer.

But it also had a U-shaped notch cut out below the ankle (an idea initially designed by Hatfield for the Air Gauntlet of 1998) to improve the fit around the heel while, tests indicated, allowing for some stretch in the upper, so that the foot was closely but comfortably and flexibly supported. And it had the seamless interior of 1999's Air Zoom Drive. The Presto also had an upper made from neoprene mesh, following the use of neoprene in the Huarache of 1991.

Neoprene was used in the Huarache to keep heat in. But later versions of the Presto looked to ways to let the heat out, replacing the neoprene with a breathable, stretchy, heat- and moisture-wicking 3D wonder material called spacer mesh – a first in footwear design – more commonly used in the medical industry, and flexible enough that the deep V-notch was no longer required. The shoe also proved an ideal platform for Nike's incoming tech, the likes of the Lunarlon sole or Flyknit upper.

In keeping with the madcap marketing of its launch, subsequent versions of the Presto would also come in denim or with a Hello Kitty print (thanks to the Japanese designer Hiroshi Fujiwara) and include special-edition collaborations with the German design house Acronym, as well as British musician Eric Clapton and the hit TV series *Sex and the City*. The Presto certainly caught the imagination of other designers: in 2017, as part of his The Ten project with Nike, Virgil Abloh deconstructed the Presto, turning it inside out, effectively adding back the seams that had so carefully been taken away; and in 2019 Rei Kawakubo gave the Presto a bonded jersey and knit profile and a rubberized tongue.

The nuttiness would resurface, too: seeing scope for the Presto to become the shoe of a new urban sport by the name of parkour, a 2002 commercial showed the French free-runner Sébastien Foucan being pursued relentlessly around the city – by an angry chicken.

Air Trainer 1

The Air Trainer 1 was not a shoe that Nike ever planned to actually make. It was a prototype, but one that just happened to find its way to John McEnroe in 1986, all the more strangely since, as the tennis star has noted, 'It had nothing to do with tennis whatsoever.'

But, for McEnroe, the shoe embodied all that he wanted: support, bounce and something in which he could train across multiple scenarios. Low-tops seemed outdated, McEnroe reckoned, and hi-tops seemed too high for his purposes, but this strange mid-top suited all occasions. However, Nike didn't want McEnroe to have the shoe. McEnroe, personifying the rebellious nature that Nike claimed to foster, told them he was going to have it anyway.

'It was a jaw-dropping experience for me because I didn't know [McEnroe] was going to wear them. He wasn't supposed to. He just did it,' the shoe's designer, Tinker Hatfield, once recalled, echoing Nike's famous tagline.

Hatfield had realized just how many pairs of different shoes he was carrying around to meet all his needs – a work-out, followed by a racket sport, then maybe a run home. Reckoning he was not alone in being tired of this, he figured on creating the first 'cross trainer' – a shoe that worked well for most sports.

It had its oddities: 'No one could figure out what the strap was all about,' McEnroe has noted (though it suited his superstitious preference for tightly fitting shoes, 'so much that I would feel that I was wasn't getting enough circulation'). And not everyone appreciated the all-in-one design. Nike's marketing department is said to have referred to it as a 'pretty stupid project' that would only serve to cut into sales from other categories.

Hatfield had a hard time pitching what he described as a shoe that is 'going to sit down the middle, where it's good enough for most people'. In some sense that wasn't in keeping with the Nike spirit. But he ploughed ahead regardless and, by 1987, the Air Trainer Hi was launched – with one style in what would become a signature shade of chlorophyl green – to a mixed reception.

Athletes, professional and amateur, got the idea, but the wider public struggled, assuming – since it had been embraced by McEnroe, and then by Andre Agassi – that it was a tennis shoe. The Air Trainer's

third iteration changed that, featuring in the 'Bo Knows' commercial with baseball star Vincent 'Bo' Jackson in 1988. Surprisingly to Nike, the shoe then found a life of its own, being adopted by skateboarders, too.

Indeed, the multipurpose shoe may now be considered more of a retro style. Its layered materials make for a product that is inefficient by the more modern standards of knitted uppers. But it would, nonetheless, be the first of many in a new category.

Air Dunk

When the Dunk High was released in 1985, superficially, Peter Moore's design may have seemed all too familiar. Seemingly a mash-up of the Terminator, Legend, Air Force 1 and Air Jordan 1, onlookers might have been forgiven for wondering what was new.

Nike's 'Be true to your school' campaign pitched the shoe at college basketball teams, just as basketball was making a real impression as a college sport. And while the Dunk was appreciated on court for the stability it offered while pivoting, it was a simple aesthetic detail that made the shoe a hit off court.

LEFT: John McEnroe wearing his signature shoe, the Air Trainer 1.

With every college team signed up to use the Dunk (or the College Color High, as it was initially going to be called) came a new colourway of Dunk. And with the design of the shoe focused on large panels of colour blocking, and those panels offering the versatility for different kinds of colour blocking, too, the Dunk quickly found casual appeal. While the shoe's shape was particularly simple and wearable – something that has allowed it to stand the test of time, becoming, in effect, a generic shape – the variety of colours allowed it to still be individualistic.

This was only underscored by the Dunk's later adoption by the world of skateboarding, then still considered alternative, at least relative to mainstream sports. Nike's more deliberate early attempts to embrace skateboarding had been pretty dire, with its run of skateboard-specific models – the likes of the Schimp, Snack and Choad – largely going ignored. The strange choice of names did not help.

Rather, as the Dunk crested in popularity in basketball – replaced by more advanced shoes – and began a steady exit from the mainstream, in came skateboarding to elevate it again throughout the 1990s. This was, in large part, helped by the launch of a Dunk Low, at least for the regional

RIGHT: Blue Ivy Carter wearing Dunks.

ABOVE: The Air
Dunk.

markets of Japan and the US west coast. These
markets were freer to push the boundaries on
colours and materials, and work on collaborations,
such as the one in 1999 with American hip-hop
collective Wu-Tang. The fledging internet drove
fierce trading of these more exclusive models.

One outcome of this more localized experimentation
was the Dunk Pro B, with its fat tongue and extra
padding – a godsend for skateboarders. When Nike
caught on to their popularity with skateboarders, it
started with shoes that were technically different
from the Dunk, but they looked very similar. In 2002
it released the new Nike SB line for skateboarders
(under Nike executive Sandy Bodecker) with more
support in the footbed and heel, a new sock-liner
and so on, with later shoes bringing further
skateboarding-friendly enhancements.

A series of four Dunk Low Pro SB colourschemes were launched on Nike's signing of its first skate team and capitalized on the Dunk's colourful character as one of their main selling points – it was called the 'Colors By' series. Collaborations with skate brands – the likes of Stüssy, Zoo York, Slam City Skates among them – not only further drove the Dunk's popularity (and collectability), they also, arguably, drove the mass-market association between sneaker and street culture. By now, the style's ardent fans were coining their own nicknames for the more in-demand colours – 'Shark', 'Hulk', 'Jedi' and 'Heineken' among them – with certain colour schemes, the likes of Viotech and What The Dunk, attaining almost mythical status.

While the Dunk's appeal as a more general lifestyle shoe waxed and waned, the hype could be huge: when the Dunk Low Pro SB 'Pigeon', a collaboration with sneakerhead Jeff Staple, was released in 2005 in New York, the police had to intervene to stop a riot. Likewise, when, during the mid-to-late 2010s, the likes of Rei Kawakubo, Virgil Abloh and American rapper Travis Scott all created their own versions, the Dunk was back again, now as much a cultural artefact as a sneaker.

Air Huarache

As one billboard advertisement for the Air Huarache would have it, 'Yo, Buck Rogers, your running shoe is ready'. Yet the futuristic look of the style – designed by Tinker Hatfield and launched in 1991 – perhaps belies its intention. This was not to add lots of bells and whistles, but to strip a shoe back to its most basic, super-lightweight elements, in keeping with the trend of the time for barefoot running and as comfortable as going barefoot. Hence the shoe's name, after the super-comfortable traditional Mexican woven sandal.

The result was so different to anything Nike had released before – not least in even being free of the company's Swoosh branding – that it really wasn't sure what the reaction would be, such that it held back on proceeding with production until the very last minute. Would Nike be able to convey the idea that, in insulating, containing and protecting the foot, there could, as Hatfield argued, actually be more freedom of movement?

Hatfield's inspiration came from water-skiing. 'I remember popping my feet into a slalom ski, which has a neoprene bootie,' he has said. 'Just as I got inked out of the water, I had a vision about how it would be great for a shoe. The next morning I [sketched it].' The resulting Huarache has an upper made from close-fitting neoprene – 'Have you hugged your foot today?' as one 1992 campaign put it – with an exoskeleton saddle to support it.

RIGHT: American actor Will Smith wearing Air Huaraches in *The Fresh Prince of Bel-Air*.

Nike need not have worried – the Huarache was an immediate hit, at least with the marathon runners to whom the first 5,000 pairs were sold. Their appeal to runners was underpinned by a commercial starring the sprinter Michael Johnson.

Inevitably, however – since the same story is true of so many Nike shoes – it would be a pop-culture embrace that would make the style a much bigger success. The Huarache would become the go-to choice for Jerry Seinfeld on his TV show, and for Will Smith on *The Fresh Prince of Bel-Air*.

The resulting sales boost paved the way for subsequent versions of the style, among them the Air Huarache International (1992), the Air Flight Huarache of the same year (bringing a more streamlined boot to basketball), the Eric Avar-designed Air Zoom Huarache (2004; basketball star Kobe Bryant's choice before he got his own signature line) and the Nike Huarache Free (2011).

As one amusing ad for the style put it, in a nod to the shoe's origin: 'In ancient Mayan civilization, basketball was a game played to the death by crazed, savage warriors who grabbed and scratched and kicked and clawed each other to the delight of thousands of delirious, bloodthirsty spectators. Although the game hasn't changed much, the shoes have.'

Air Yeezy

'Nike is the number one sneaker lifestyle brand, right? And I'm the number one most influential cultural pop art brand,' announced Kanye West in 2009 without any false modesty. 'So you take those two things and you mesh that – it's very exciting. I'm the Nike of culture.'

And so began one of the most talked about collaborations in Nike's history – one that would spark an interest in sneakers for a new generation: the Air Yeezy. This was teased in prototype form by West at the Grammys in 2008 (this pair would later set a record for the most expensive sneaker sold at auction) and launched the following year.

BELOW: The Air Yeezy 2.

The first edition was developed by West sitting with Tinker Hatfield, the then creative director Mark Smith and designer Tiffany Beers in Nike's Innovation Center and, as West put it, 'vibing it out . . . Every guy drew Nikes in fourth grade, so to really do it is a dream come true.'

Of course, at that point, Nike could not have known that, in time, West would jump ship for a reported US$10 million deal – plus better royalties – to Adidas. That Nike was not West's first sneaker collaboration (that had been with the Japanese streetwear label BAPE in 2005) and that in 2009 he had also signed to design sneakers for Louis Vuitton, might have suggested that Nike was unlikely to be his last stop.

Yet, in the meantime, West *et al.* would pull together what the rapper hoped would be a 'shoe-like space boot, made for a person that's walking on another planet', with a relatively monotone exterior (that is, after considering several hundred colour combinations), perforated uppers, plenty of pop colour on the liner and glow-in-the-dark soles. The original idea of developing a unique sole for the shoe had to be abandoned (in favour of using an off-the-shelf Air bubble sole) because it was taking too long. That, West said, broke his heart.

But not enough that he wouldn't follow up with the Air Yeezy 2 in 2012, co-designed with Nike's Nathan VanHook and based around Andre Agassi's Tech

Challenge 2 – though even the flamboyant tennis star would likely not have got away with reptilian scales and Egyptian hieroglyphics. Perhaps the most famous version of this model was that dubbed the Red October, quietly released in 2014 some months after West had left for Germany and, maybe for that very reason, selling out in a matter of minutes, with at least one pair promptly relisted on eBay with a hopeful buy-it-now price of US$16.3 million.

Blazer

The Blazer may be uncomplicated, both stylistically and technologically, compared to what Nike would produce over the years following its launch in 1973, but back then it represented a major milestone in the company's history. Created by runners to make running shoes, Nike knew that growth would necessitate designing shoes for other sports. It would mean taking on Converse and Adidas in sports in which they were not just well-established but also historically resonant.

The Blazer, then, was Nike's first non-running shoe, and its first basketball boot. It was also a statement of intent: just 13 years later, Nike would launch the Air Jordan 1, the shoe that would, effectively, win basketball for the brand. That is perhaps why Nike made a point of sizing up its Swoosh branding on the Blazer, so that it could be seen on players' feet at a distance, and on TV, and maybe prompt the question, 'What are those?'

ABOVE: The Blazer.

The Blazer was named after Nike's hometown basketball team, the Portland Trail Blazers. It was, as the company described it, a 'traditional bulb-toe shoe . . . built for action and durability'. It trumpeted its padded ankle collar, exposed poly-foam tongue, sponge arch support and Terry cloth insole – all cutting-edge for the time. Other aspects were borrowed. Early versions had a rubber shell toe, just like Adidas's Superstar – launched two years before. And, like the Converse Chuck Taylor, it was produced in both high- and low-top formats. Again, like Converse – which produced its basketball footwear in coloured canvas for the first time in 1971, so teams could coordinate their uniforms – Nike launched the Blazer in a variety of colours, too.

It would take five years from launching before Nike could sign up an NBA player to endorse the shoe. That was the San Antonio Spurs player George Gervin who, for added sweetness, switched to Nike from Adidas. Later, Gervin was blunt about his reasons for switching: 'Nike was very innovative. [It] was thinking out of the box back in the 1970s. It was a better-quality shoe,' he said in a YouTube video with Nice Kicks. Then he added: 'I used to wear Adidas and then Nike approached me and wanted to give me much more money.' In an early example of what the signature shoe would become – the Blazer is possibly the very first Player Exclusive (PE) model – Gervin's had his nickname, Iceman, stamped across the heel.

Eventually eclipsed by new basketball shoes, in the mid-1990s the Blazer's rugged leather upper and vulcanized rubber sole grip would give it a second life as skateboarding's more underground choice, much as the Dunk would also do later once it had fallen from favour. Nike embraced the opportunity, in 2005 signing up the American pro skateboarder Lance Mountain to redesign the Blazer with skateboarding more in mind – by adding an Air sole, for instance. By then, the Blazer had become a focal point for collaborations that only served to underscore its reborn credibility, with Stüssy (in 2002), Futura 2000 (2003) and Supreme – which rendered the Nike Swoosh in a quilted faux snakeskin in 2006 – among others.

Air Foamposite One

The Air Foamposite One turned how footwear was constructed on its head and managed to upset the dominance of the endless parade of Jordans in basketball. However, designer Eric Avar and the Advanced Products Engineering team at Nike struggled to get the go-ahead to take what he called its 'pure experimentation' – a shoe inspired by a beetle's shell – into prototyping.

Traditionally, shoes were made by stitching leather panels together. The idea for the Foamposite was to mould the entire upper in one seamless piece using a plastic-based, polyurethane liquid material poured at a very high temperature into a mould – a first in footwear design, resulting in an all-round, foot-embracing fit. However, this was not cheap. Sometimes even great ideas are just too expensive, too complex to market, too strange – at least for the times – to work.

Certainly, Nike had to ask around to find an engineering contractor who thought they could fulfil the brief. Many said they couldn't. Finally, Daewoo, the South Korean car company, offered to use its production systems for Nike, meaning the footwear giant didn't have to invest in specialist equipment for a product that might not, in the end, make commercial sense. All the same, it did mean Nike

RIGHT: Penny Hardaway playing for Orlando Magic in 1999.

ABOVE: The Air
Foamposite One.

had to pay Daewoo US$750,000 for the mould alone. Eventually, the Foamposite got the green light and was launched in 1997, four years after the idea was first mooted.

Initially, the style proved divisive and did not sell well, perhaps encouraging Nike to seek a return on its investment, applying the Posite upper technology to a number of subsequent styles through to 2000, including the Total Air Foamposite Max, the Air Flightposite and the oddity that was the Clogposite.

There were some bold colour choices for the Foamposite itself, including: pewter, which made the shoe look like it was made from the liquid metal that featured in *Terminator 2* (1991); weatherman, which made the upper akin to a meteorological map; and (the biggest hit) galaxy, something akin to a photograph of distant star systems from the Hubble Space Telescope. Colour, indeed, would be central to the Foamposite's story.

Following the shoe's launch, it was by chance that Nike would soon find an NBA star to wear what was, on the face of it, an unconventional, to some eyes odd-looking, and certainly futuristic shoe. Orlando Magic player Penny Hardaway already had his own signature shoe, the Air Penny 1. But when he saw the Foamposite – a sample sticking out of Avar's bag at an 'innovation meeting' around 1995 – he is said to have simply proclaimed, 'That's it!' and requested that it be his next shoe.

He got more than he bargained for. Arriving in a shiny royal-blue upper and mounted on that bulbous outsole, it wasn't just the weirdness that his team management weren't sure about – the colour didn't match the team uniform. Hardaway came up with a simple solution – he coloured in the upper with a black permanent marker, a moment in Nike lore later marked by the issue in 2015 of the Air Foamposite One 'Sharpie' colourway.

Curiously, Nike didn't think there would be much likelihood of ever reissuing the Foamposite One, so it destroyed the original moulds. But, inevitably, a forgotten shoe is reimagined by fashion. A collaboration with Supreme in 2014 is said to have seen the NYPD order the streetwear brand to cancel its in-store launch to avoid a potential riot, so the style was sold online only. In 2021 Comme des Garçons, meanwhile, took the opportunity to rework the upper mould to create a swirling contoured effect said to be inspired by sand patterns in a traditional Japanese garden.

Air Max

The Air Max 1 was not the first shoe to carry Nike's 'air bubble' Air outsole technology (that was the 1979 Tailwind), and yet it has come to represent it, in no small part because this was the shoe that, with its launch on 26 March 1987, made the technology visible.

Not everyone at Nike loved the idea: its designer, Tinker Hatfield, has said that management thought 'I had pushed [the shoe's look] too far.' Some, he said, even wanted to fire him. He argued that it would finally allow consumers to understand what Nike's much-trumpeted Air technology actually meant (see Nike Air, pages 76–80).

Such is the cultishness of this shoe that sneaker fanatics even celebrate Air Max Day each year on 26 March. That's when the latest styles are revealed by Nike, typically to buying panic, given how various Max iterations over the years have boldly moved the line on. Among these have been the likes of the 90, also designed by Hatfield; Sergio Lozano's black midsoled and speed-laced 95, with graduated striations inspired by the walls of the Grand Canyon; and the 97, by Christian Tresser (until then a designer focused on

RIGHT: American film director Spike Lee wearing the Air Max 1.

football boots for Nike), inspired by the Japanese bullet train and the aluminium and polished titanium finishes of mountain bikes of that time.

Each year tended to see a new technological step, too. The Hatfield-designed Air Max 93 used a neoprene collar – the designer having experimented with neoprene for the Huarache. Designer Sean McDowell's Air Max Plus (1998) introduced what was called 'Tuned Air', the sole displaying a series of individual Air cushions, each calibrated to differing pressures. There was the Air VaporMax (2017), the first Nike shoe to be free of foam and rubber in the mid *and* outsole, the upper being fused directly onto the air bag. And the Air Max Scorpion (2022), offering more air cushioning than any other Nike shoe to date, in terms of pounds per square inch, and with an outrageous sole aesthetic to boot.

As the Air Max line advanced, the looks of the shoes were not always in keeping with the streamlined style of the Air Max 1. And yet, just as the Air Max name has held these disparate shoes together, so

BELOW: The Air Vapormax.

each model would speak to a different subculture. If the Jordan brand would explode such that it had a life of its own apart from Nike, so the Air Max would become singularly resonant in a similar way.

It has chimed from the UK grime scene of Skepta and Dizzee Rascal (on the cover of his *Boy in da Corner* album of 2003) to the hip-hop of Redman and The Game. Go to France, and the Air Max Plus was nicknamed 'Le Requin', or 'The Shark'. Go to Italy, and ravers of the 1990s nicknamed the Air Max 97 'Le Silver' for its metallic finish – by one account, sales of the 97 in Italy were greater than the rest of the world combined. This was, no doubt, inspired by Nike's TV commercial for the Italian market in which a Viking king offers the American athlete Quincy Watts his large wife in exchange for Watts' shoes: 'The super-cushioned wife for your super-cushioned Air Max Nikes.'

Air Jordan

The Air Jordan is the sneaker juggernaut. There's its back-story – Nike's gamble in wooing Michael Jordan in 1984, and how the deal changed sports marketing forever (see pages 67–71); and the huge sales it and other Jordan brand products would generate – making Jordan a billionaire and repaying Nike's investment countless times over. All this aside, the sneaker would merit special attention just for the love it's shown by its fans, and for its longevity.

While certain models may often be cited as among the best in class – the Air Jordan 1, 3 and 4, and Hatfield's P-51 Mustang fighter plane-inspired Jordan 5, 6 and 11 among them – there have, at the time of writing, been 37 editions of the Jordan, not counting the hundreds of different colour options. Variations have dominated sneaker trading and the resale market.

But it is the first, naturally, that defined the design, with the fixed straps at the forefront and ankle for stability, the padded ankle cushions and the supportive heel cup all important to players. As for the public? What really resonated about 1985's Air Jordan 1 – as with the Dunk of the same year – was its use of colour.

It was for that reason that, when Nike released the Jordan 1, on April Fool's Day, Peter Moore's design (really a spin on Bruce Kilgore's Air Force 1s) shocked the basketball establishment. The shoe came in the Chicago Bulls' colours of white, black and red – including Nike's innovation of having home and away shoe colours. Jordan was not keen on this idea, not least because he considered red to be 'the devil's colour', having failed in his bid to have them made in blue. The NBA didn't like it either – the shoes

RIGHT: British model Jourdan Dunn wearing the Air Jordan.

FROM LEFT:
Air Jordan 3,
Air Jordan 4,
Air Jordan 5,
Air Jordan 11.

were in direct contravention of its rule stating that all footwear should be mostly black or white.

'[But] the idea was to break the colour barrier in footwear,' Moore noted, '[given that] prior to that, 99 per cent of shoes were white or black.' So, apocryphally at least, Nike simply decided that it would pay the fine of US$5,000 per game that Jordan was threatened with every time he stepped on the court.

'[The shoe] was so colourful that the NBA banned it – which was great!' Knight once enthused. 'We actually welcome the kind of publicity that pits us against the establishment, as long as we know we're on the right side of the issue.' Nike even played on that in the launch commercial: 'On September 15th, Nike created a revolutionary new basketball show. On October 18th, the NBA threw them out of the game,' it intoned. 'Fortunately, the NBA can't stop you from wearing them.'

Unfortunately, Jordan didn't actually wear his new namesake basketball shoes on 18 October – he wore

a pair of Nike Air Ships, a stylistic stopgap of sorts between Air Force 1s and Air Jordan 1s. He wouldn't wear Air Jordan 1s on court until November, something Nike, to preserve the myth, has kept quiet about ever since, even as, in 2021, a pair of Jordan 'game-worn' Air Ships became the first sneaker to achieve over a million dollars at auction, finally selling for US$1.5 million. What's more, while sneaker collectors still refer to the Air Jordan 1 as 'banned', this is disputed: it's also said that the first Jordans actually worn on court had enough white in their design to be within NBA rules.

Does this matter? Not to the myth or to the brand. The Jordan shoe still stands apart because, in many ways, it is under Nike's wing but quickly became distinct from it. After all, if Nike is the Swoosh, a pair of Jordans even have their own Peter Moore-designed winged basketball and (from 3 onwards) Jumpman logos – the latter created in 1997 and adapted from a *Life* magazine photograph of Michael Jordan, mid-flight and ball in hand.

Epilogue

Nike thinks of itself as a sportswear company – and it is in maintaining that ethos that the American giant has its impressive track record of design innovation, its deep ties with the biggest stars in sport and a number of products that can rightly be considered design classics.

But, of course, Nike is so much more than that. For one, it has ridden a wave that it helped to shape. This is a wave that has seen two forces intersect: the rise of streetwear as the dominant form of fashion, and a new emphasis on practicality and comfort in the way we dress. That's why, while Nike is a footwear company before anything else – it's in footwear that most of its big ideas find a home – it's also, more broadly, an apparel company, able to charge a premium by putting its Swoosh on basic clothing styles that many people now regard as central to their wardrobes, outside of work and, increasingly, inside work, too.

Secondly, Nike has become a kind of cult, with its devoted adherents hanging on the release date for every new shoe, and having indirectly birthed an entire parallel economy devoted to the resale of its most desirable designs. That these sneakers often achieve stupendous prices, that they are increasingly considered an asset, perhaps tells us all we need to know about Nike's future.

Yes, there will be many more competitors to come. But few can only dream of having the impact – on engineering, on sport and on culture – of Nike.

Index

Picture Credits

First published in Great Britain in 2024 by
Laurence King
An imprint of Quercus Editions Ltd
Carmelite House
50 Victoria Embankment
London EC4Y 0DZ
An Hachette UK company

A CIP catalogue record for this book is available from the British Library

HB ISBN 9781529438666
Ebook ISBN 9781529438673

10 9 8 7 6 5

Cover design and art direction: Luke Bird
Design: Ginny Zeal
Commissioning editors: Nicole Thomas and Sophie Wise
Project manager and editor: Victoria Lympus
Printed and bound in Italy by L.E.G.O. S.p.A.

Papers used by Quercus are from well-managed forests and other responsible sources.